MW01443767

THE MISFIT MILLIONAIRE

THE LIFE AND TIMES OF TERRY DUPERON

DONALD STEELE, PH.D

Copyright © 2022 by Steele PhD LLC

All rights reserved.

No part of this book may be reproduced in any form or by any electronic or mechanical means, including information storage and retrieval systems, without written permission from the author, except for the use of brief quotations in a book review.

To my grandchildren and great-grandchildren:

In this book I have tried to be as transparent as possible — the good and the bad, the successes and failures — in order to give you a clear picture of my life and times. I hope this book leaves you with hope for a better future; that you pursue your dreams; that you find a mate and a career that will fulfill your life; that you find God early, earlier than I did; and that you learn to love and be loved. God has always turned the very worst things in my life into the very best things that ever happened to me. I love my life and I have for a very long time.

Terry Duperon

CONTENTS

Run With What You've Got   vii

1. The Portrait of a Misfit?   1
2. Shifting from Desperation to Inspiration   12
3. Muddling Through   22
4. Farm Boy in the City   29
5. Lonely Together   44
6. When the Going Gets Tough   57
7. The Next Clear Step: Divorce   66
8. Climbing the Career Ladder   77
9. A Profound Transformation   91
10. Terry Enters the Entrepreneurial World   106
11. Leslie and Terry's Courtship   119
12. Here Comes the Bride   141
13. The "Eighteen and Out" Rule   153
14. Capturing Government Contracts   164
15. A Turn For The Better   177
16. An Unbelievable Window of Opportunity   191

17. What Goes Up Must Come Down	204
18. Teamwork Makes the Dream Work	211
19. The "You and Me" Culture	225
20. The CLASS	241
21. The Pursuit of Happiness	249
Appendix	255
About the Author	259
Acknowledgments	261

RUN WITH WHAT YOU'VE GOT

The Dalai Lama says, "The purpose of our lives is to be happy." In life, however, the pursuit of happiness can be very elusive for a person born with a learning disability. Terry Duperon discovered he couldn't read like the rest of the kids while in his third-grade class. Asked to read a first-grade book entitled *Dick and Jane*, he simply couldn't do it. He would later learn, at the age of forty-seven, that he has dyslexia disorder. This disorder is characterized by difficulty reading. It occurs with children of normal vision and intelligence. Before this disorder was diagnosable, those like Terry were generally viewed as mentally deficient. This disorder made Terry feel like, and in many ways behave as, a misfit.

What is a misfit? A misfit is a person whose behaviors and attitudes set him apart from others in an uncomfortable and conspicuous way — a fish out of water; a square peg in a round hole; or simply a non-conformist.

It is important to note that as Terry was growing up, he had no meaningful misfit role model. More recently, the role of a madcap spiritual godmother to little misfits like Terry is one that Lady Gaga has down cold. Terry had no roadmap, no coaching, and no clear path to follow.

Fortunately, Terry functioned very well on the Indiantown farm on which he was raised, even though he got little praise from his father. As Terry says, "Dad was a hot-headed Frenchman who never gave me 'atta-boys.' But he did show confidence in my ability to work with machinery."

Albert Einstein offers, "If you want to live a happy life, tie it to a goal [or a dream], not to people or things." What propelled Terry forward, despite many challenges, was his dream that if he could create one useful invention, he would become a successful inventor.

Terry's dream evolved over time to his wanting to become an inventor so successful that he could live a lifestyle like Henry Ford and gain the dignity and respect he failed to get as a youngster. The seed was planted in his subconscious mind. Once planted, that seed would blossom and bear fruit. Living in pursuit of his dream, one clear step at a time, proved to be the needed nutrient to enrich the soil and grow that seed.

Terry coupled this dream with creativity, perseverance, and hard work. He discovered early on that life works out the best for those who make the best of how things work out.

Perhaps Terry's unique quality is that he's insatiably curious, a quality that fuels his passion for invention. It was auspicious to approach any situation from a deferential inquisitive place.

This book is the third in a series of legacy books I am writing. Each of us has a compelling story to tell about our lives. As I interview people about their experiences, I find it strange the things they remember: the people, the places, the moments in time, bound to their hearts while others have faded into the mist.

Terry acknowledged early on in our initial conversations that he always knew he lived a life different from most other people. In his words, "When I was a child, I saw no path before me. All I had was a dream, a vague notion of what I wanted my life to be like. My dream pulled me forward while so many other things were holding me back."

To this day, Terry lives by the following mantras: *Run with what you've got,* and *Never be the one who holds you back.*

The Electric Light Orchestra (ELO) recorded and released the following song that really relates to this theme:

Hold on Tight to Your Dream

> *Hold on tight to your dream*
> *Hold on tight to your dream*
> *When you see your ship go*
>   *sailing*

*When you feel your heart is
    breaking
Hold on tight to your dream*

*It's a long time to be gone
Time just rolls on and on
When you need a shoulder to
    cry on
When you get so sick of trying
Hold on tight to your dream*

*When you get so down that you
    can't get up
And you want so much but you're
    all out of luck
When you're so downhearted and
    misunderstood
Just over and over you could*

*Hold on tight to your dream
Hold on tight to your dream
When you see the shadows
    falling
When you hear the cold wind
    calling
Hold on tight to your dream*

This book unfolds the song of Terry Duperon's pursuit of happiness. It is a raw and revealing portrait of a profound transformation from misfit to successful entrepreneur. His message to readers, especially those who may see themselves as misfits, is "Run with what you've got."

1

THE PORTRAIT OF A MISFIT?

Terry discovered early on that he was a misfit. In his words, "I couldn't read, I wasn't good in school, I wasn't good at sports, and socially I just didn't fit in. In most ways, I was a misfit." As I listened to Terry, I was reminded of a question comedian George Goble asked Johnny Carson on *The Tonight Show* (1969):

Did you ever get the feeling that the world was a tuxedo and you were a pair of brown shoes?

In 1990, at the age of forty-seven, Terry learned that he is dyslexic. He was informed of the term "dyslexia" by a Saginaw Valley State University professor that had a son who was dyslexic. Terry felt a sense of relief that enabled him to stop hiding his condition. And then he was surprised at the lack of negative reaction when he openly revealed his condition to others. Up until that revelation, he had always known that something wasn't right. He thought, "Perhaps I am just dumber than the other kids in school." In a word, Terry felt *marginalized* in many situations — placed in a position of little importance, influence, or power. Sometimes he wondered, "Am I crazy?"

No one is a misfit in all situations. For example, I have coached and counseled many professional athletes and entertainers. A great athlete may fit in very well within the confines of the locker room and on the field of play, but may be a misfit in social situations. Terry's dyslexia is a developmental disorder that can affect many aspects of a person's life, including language, learning mobility, and independence.

Let's look at what dyslexia is and what it is not. Dyslexia is just one of a myriad of misfit conditions. It is interesting to note that a staggering 5 to 15 percent of Americans — 14.5 to

43.5 million children and adults — have dyslexia.

In America, dyslexia is referred to most commonly as a disability and it is generally treated that way in our school systems. In contrast, in Europe, dyslexia is referred to as a "specific learning difference." This definition leads to more exploration of how to diagnose and treat learning differences. This distinction is a significant one because where a difference can be overcome, a disability describes a lifelong incapacity.

Dyslexia impacts a person's reading and spelling ability, yet has nothing to do with intelligence. While dyslexic people have difficulty reading, they are often extremely creative individuals who excel at seeing the big picture, finding patterns, and bringing together information from different domains. They may be visually-spatially oriented and are often talented musicians and artists who tend to be dynamic problem solvers who think out of the box. They have magical brains. They simply process information differently.

In fact, many successful dyslexics see dyslexia as their greatest strength and they attribute their enhanced creativity and problem-solving skills to the unique way in which they process information. Consider the following words from a few famous dyslexics:

- If anyone ever puts you down for being dyslexic, don't believe them. Being dyslexic can actually be an advantage, and it has certainly helped me.

  — Richard Branson, Virgin CEO

- I never read in school. I got bad grades — Ds and Fs and some Cs in some classes. In the second week of the eleventh grade, I just quit. Everything I learned, I just learned by listening.

  — Cher, actress and singer

- My teachers told my mother that I was addled [mentally deficient]. My father thought I was stupid, and I almost believed I was a dunce.

— Thomas Edison, inventor

- I read so slowly. If I have a script, I'm going to read it five times over.

— Channing Tatum, actor

- It's more common than you can imagine. You are not alone.

— Steven Spielberg, director

Other famous dyslexics include Jay Leno, Jennifer Aniston, Whoopi Goldberg, Pablo Picasso, Tom Cruise, Mohammed Ali, Nolan Ryan, Albert Einstein, and many more.

We might include Terry Duperon on the above list of successful dyslexics. Through his no-holds-barred truth-telling, Terry pulls the curtain back on his trials and tribulations, successes and failures, and reveals his tortured path to becoming a successful business founder and inventor, pulled along by his dream of living a lifestyle like Henry Ford. Above all, he wanted to gain the dignity and respect he was deprived of in his middle and high school years.

While stories of these successful dyslexics are truly inspiring, it must not be lost that this is not always the case. School life can be extremely painful and frustrating to a child or young adult when they can't learn to read.

The emotional struggles from being a misfit can be extremely damaging to a child's self-esteem. Unlike physical damage, emotional damage is often overlooked. From my experience working with children and youth, they would rather get a black eye than suffer emotionally.

The most common form of dyslexia interrupts a student's ability to split words into their component sounds. This makes sounding out words very difficult. To quote one of my dyslexic clients, "Teaching a dyslexic to read is like trying to teach a pig to sing. First, it's aggravating to the pig; and secondly, it's never going to sound good anyway."

Fortunately, there are programs and methodologies on the rise in American schools that are dedicated to helping dyslexic children learn to read without damaging the student's self-image. Fast ForWord is one of the best-known programs and it touts a very high success rate in helping dyslexics and others with learning differences. In the Great Lakes Bay Region of Michigan where Terry grew up, the Orton-Gillingham Foundation is helping children and youth with reading skills.

Learning is one of the most fundamental core competencies we need as human beings. Fortunately, we are created as learning systems. It is innate. Children have a sense of wonder about the world — an approach to living in inquiry, always looking for what could be. As adults, we tend to lose this sense of wonder and stop living in inquiry as children do.

My view as a former urban school superintendent of schools in Saginaw, Michigan; Toledo, Ohio; and Seattle, Washington, is that school districts have become far too attached to a teach-test-teach model focused mainly on reading and math, and tested through programs like MEAP (Michigan Educational Assessment Program). If school districts are to shift to different methodologies and outcomes that meet the needs of all children and youth, including misfits, they must focus more on *how we learn* (i.e., the thought patterns of high performance people) and less on *what we need to learn.*

This leads me to suggest that politicians and school district leadership should focus on looking more broadly and deeply into the research of people like Harvard University Professor Howard Gardner. In his book *Frames of Mind* (1983), Gardner originally defined seven intelligences to capture the diverse abilities and talents that people possess. Gardner theorized that people do not have only an intellectual capacity, they have many kinds of intelligence, including, but not limited to:

- Linguistic (word smart)
- Logical (mathematical, numerical, reasoning, logic intelligence)
- Bodily/Kinesthetic (physically smart)
- Musical (music smart)
- Interpersonal (people smart)

- Intrapersonal (self smart)
- Naturalist (nature smart)

Gardner has now expanded his list to include visual-spatial. Visual-spatial intelligence is a human computational capacity that provides the ability or mental skill to solve spatial problems of navigation; visualization of objects from different angles; space, face, or scene recognition; or to notice fine details. This is a special intelligence that Terry possesses. It is his gift.

If the schools back in the 1950s and 60s (or today, for that matter) had tested for visual-spatial intelligence (as well as others), Terry might have graduated as valedictorian of his class rather than suffering the humiliation foisted upon him by forcing him to function and test solely in the linguistic and mathematical domains.

Terry's visual-spatial intelligence plays well into his daydreaming ability. Daydreaming is the stream of consciousness that detaches from current external tasks when attention drifts to a more personal and internal direction. This phenomenon is common in people's daily life, shown by a large-scale study in which participants spend on average 47 percent of their waking time daydreaming. To quote from the article "So, Is Daydreaming Good For Us?" by Stefan Van der Stigchel, "Scientists at Harvard have developed an app that can be used to ask test subjects what they are doing at any given moment during the day. The technique is called *experience sampling*. In experiments, test subjects were also asked whether they felt happy at that particular moment. The scientists are still collecting additional data, but a whopping 2,250 people took part in the first study, so they have already compiled a massive amount — approximately 250,000 measurements."

Based on the results of that study, it is more than reasonable to assess that a student who can't read will spend an inordinate amount of time staring out the window daydreaming about more exciting, more relatable things. That would be Terry.

Let's offer a toast to the genius of Terry Duperon and other misfits!

Let's offer a toast to the crazy ones. The misfits. The rebels. The troublemakers. The round pegs in square holes. The ones who see the world differently. They are not fond of rules and they have no respect for the status quo. You can quote them, disagree with them, glorify or vilify them. About the only thing you can't do is ignore them, because they change things. They push the human race forward. And while some may see them as the crazy ones, it is also possible to see them as geniuses. The people who are crazy enough to think they can change the world are the ones who do it.

2

SHIFTING FROM DESPERATION TO INSPIRATION

Conventional wisdom and many studies support the premise that, during the first six years of life, children who are nurtured to believe themselves to be safe, loved, and capable will do well in school. However, even having the childhood beliefs that one is safe, loved, and capable are not enough to accommodate and meet the needs of children whom I am calling misfits. Why use this

Edward Duperon

name? Because they are in some ways different from, but clearly not less than, other children, and they must find different ways to navigate through their educational and social lives than those avenues available to most children.

Terry was the last of seven children, born to Edward and Luella (Lou) Duperon on September 2, 1943. The Duperon family worked the fields on their small farm located in Indiantown, a farming community located about nine miles northeast of downtown Saginaw, Michigan.

His dad and mom were hard-working, frugal people. According to Terry, "Dad was a hot-headed Frenchman whose temper was easily and frequently brought to a boil. He was simply a man's man and a product of the fears and anxieties caused by living through the Great Depression. Dad was in charge and never let

Lou Duperon

any of us children forget that he was the king."

Lou was the homemaker, but she frequently worked the fields alongside Edward. Terry recalls some fond memories he shared with his mom when he was around five years old: "Mom took me out to the garden. We were positioned on our knees, facing each other. I can still see the brown house dress she was wearing. It had big white flowers on it. She cut each of us a piece of melon and we just knelt there quietly. It was such a wonderful feeling.

"On another occasion, Mom and I sat at the kitchen table eating cinnamon toast. With seven kids in the family, and me being the youngest, these times spent alone with my mother are still precious. I loved my mom and I guess she saw me as her baby and probably her last child."

When Terry's dad and mom would work in the fields, they would place little Terry under a tree where they could see him. Terry remembers, "They would give me this big silver spoon to play with. Armed with only that spoon, I would dig shallow ditches, plant little twigs as if they were trees, build bridges, and try to create little villages."

Terry on the family farm, age two, with older brother home from WWII in background.

Terry reflects, "I knew that Dad and Mom loved each other, in spite of the fact they argued from daylight until dusk. Mom usually ended up being a calming influence in reaction to Dad's temper outbursts."

When asked if he felt safe, loved, and capable at six years of age, he said, "Yes, I always felt safe, probably because I knew my dad wouldn't take any guff from anyone and that he would always protect his family. Mom was my source of affection and she was the glue that kept the family together. And I learned early on that I was expected to do my chores, and if I did them wrong or skipped them, I was expected to fix that problem. I never, ever got off the hook. From that early beginning, I felt capable of doing what I was expected to do."

It was at the age of five that Terry entered the two-room Indiantown schoolhouse. The first room housed first- through fourth-graders (Indiantown School had no kindergarten). The second room hosted fifth- through eighth-graders. Terry's sister, Yvonne, took him to school on that first day. Terry said, "I had no idea why I was even there. Only my sister and I were still in grade school. The rest of the kids in my family were in the upper grades or already out of school."

It is hard to imagine a situation today wherein a five-year-old child would not be prepared by his parents for what he can expect to experience when he goes to school. But that was the case with Terry.

As Terry moved through the early grades, he really felt no different than any of the other kids. He loved recess and was soon looked upon as one who could and would defend himself. He was already farm-kid strong and saw himself as the king of the hill.

Indiantown School

Then two life-changing events happened during his third year in school. The first one created a feeling of desperation. It put Terry into a downward spiral. The second was inspirational, elevating Terry's spirit because it offered a vague picture of a bright future. The first trigger happened when the teacher asked Terry to read aloud in front of his classmates. Terry simply couldn't do it. As Terry puts it, "Up until third grade, I felt I was like the rest of the kids in class: not too smart, not too dumb, just one of the kids waiting for the bell to ring so we could go out for recess. But all that changed on the day my teacher asked me to stand up and read out loud. It wasn't the third-grade book she handed me. It was a first-grade book, *Dick and Jane,* and I couldn't read it. I stumbled and stammered, but when I looked up and saw the rest of the class staring at me, I suddenly knew I wasn't like the other kids.

"'Sound out the words, Terry,' the teacher told me. But I couldn't. I mean, I could see the words all right; but for me to attach a sound to a printed letter was impossible. I might as well have tried to read dog tracks. And here we were, all my classmates watching me struggle with that first-grade book.

"I looked around in complete embarrassment and concluded, 'Something is wrong with me.' I felt sick to my stomach and knew I just didn't fit in." Terry realized, for the first time at the early age of eight years old, that something was seriously wrong with him. He couldn't read words as the other kids could, no matter how hard he tried. "Everything felt different after that. I became mischievous and an exasperation to my teachers.

"Why was this happening to me? As far as I know, I was the only one in the family that had problems reading and writing. Not that it made a whole lot of difference. Heck, we were farmers trying to scrape out a living from the soil. My folks may have been a little puzzled by it, but they didn't get upset. I was doing all right working around the farm. Fact is, I was driving a tractor when most kids my age were going to the swimming hole. Reading, at least to my dad, was sort of secondary. He knew I could do a lot of things around the farm, and if I didn't know how, he expected me to learn. His unspoken message was, 'You learn by doing.' And Dad was not a patient man. If I didn't get it right the first time, you better believe I kept trying until I did.

"My dad tried to help me do better in

school by promising to buy me a new first baseman's glove that I wanted — if and only if I got 100 percent on my next two ten-word spelling tests. Even that backfired for me. Since I couldn't read the words, I spent every waking hour memorizing the pattern of the words, seeing them as a picture. The words could have been in another language and it wouldn't have made a difference to me. As long as the words were presented in the exact order that the teacher provided, I would do well on the tests. My different learning process worked. Sure enough, the teacher presented the words on the spelling tests in that same order. I got 100 percent on both tests."

Terry says, "The problem that arose was this: Now Dad and Mom were convinced that, if I only studied harder, I would do much better in school. That was not the case because I could not repeat that success on other tests. The good news was that I did get my new baseball glove."

The second trigger occurred when the teacher began to teach about famous inventors like Henry Ford, Eli Whitney, Thomas Edison, and Alexander Graham Bell. Terry listened carefully and thought to himself, "If I can become an inventor, I will live a lifestyle like Henry Ford." This thought gave birth to a dream.

Clearly, Terry was made to feel he was safe, loved, and capable at home with his hard-working family. At school, this was generally not the case. The desperation triggered by the discovery that he couldn't read was offset by his dream. "I had heard stories about how people would invent just one thing and that one thing would make them rich and famous. I had no idea of how I would get there, but I was determined to do so. The innocence and power of my childhood imagination helped me keep from living a life of despair.

"I began, early on, to try to invent things. Once, an older neighbor stopped over to see Dad. He found me enthusiastically pounding hundreds of nails into a plain old board. When he asked me what I was building, I proudly announced, 'The coming thing.'"

Terry's dream was born: *I will be an inventor and live a rich life.*

3

MUDDLING THROUGH

Terry entered the fifth grade via passing on condition. Essentially, that meant that Terry was not functioning at or near grade level. Today, we would refer to that condition as social promotion, with the goal being to keep students with their age group, hopefully giving them a chance to catch up academically. Since the big room of this two-room schoolhouse served students in grades five through eight, fifth-grader Terry was no longer looked upon as a tough guy. He didn't know that at first, but he learned quickly after losing a couple of skirmishes. Now he was not just a poor student;

he had lost his stature as king of the mountain.

Terry's primary way of coping with his inability to read was to learn by doing. His secondary way of learning was to listen carefully. Terry admits, "I never did any homework, never even took a book home. Even so, I didn't fail at everything. I learned a lot by doing and by listening. I am a good listener and still go out of my way to listen to things that I'm interested in. Just don't ask me to write a paper about it. In school, the only thing I got interested in was inventors. Just the idea of a person creating something that naturally welled up in their head fascinated me.

"Most kids my age were into Roy Rogers and Gene Autry from the movies, or Bobby Lane [Detroit Lions quarterback] and Joe DiMaggio [New York Yankees center fielder]. Not me. My heroes were all inventors."

During this span of Terry's life, he remembers Fridays as his favorite day of the week because that was the day his mom would bake bread and cinnamon rolls. Terry recalls, "I could literally smell the baking as I ran home from school. What a way to start the weekend."

Terry learned how to run farm machinery, drive a tractor, and work the fields. He was so small when he started that his feet wouldn't reach the floorboard of the tractor. By middle school, he was very adept at driving the tractor. He also discovered that he was good at tearing down machines, but when it came to putting machines back together — not so much! But he was made to learn, because his dad never let him off the hook. His dad's familiar hue and cry was, "Terry, you took it apart. Now, put it back together, just as you found it."

In a strange way, his dad was expressing confidence in Terry's ingenuity in figuring things out in his own way. His "learn-by-doing" approach to tearing apart machines and putting them back together would serve Terry in later years. His unique visual-spatial intelligence proved to be useful for getting machines of all kinds to work efficiently and effectively.

It was during this time that Terry's mechanical abilities began to develop. Since he could not read written directions, he would simply try different things until he succeeded. Simplicity of operation was central to Terry's inventions. In his words, "Two parts: one part too many!"

During this span of middle school years, Terry came to fear his dad's temper. Terry says, "I never knew what would set Dad off. He was like Jackie Gleason on the old TV show *The Honeymooners*. In that show, anything and everything would set Jackie off."

Terry remembers, "I was frequently in trouble during my middle school years. Dad would, on occasion, grab a switch off a tree and swat me across the back of my legs. This did not happen often, but when it did, I clearly deserved it. One time, Dad had given me a direct order to not cut the neighbor's grass. But when the neighbor asked me to do that, I complied. Dad went into his Jackie Gleason rage and swatted me.

"Another time, Dad was up on a scaffold, hanging wallpaper. When the left side of what he was hanging started peeling off from the wall, he swore a blue streak and moved over to that side to re-paste it. Then, the right side began to peel off. Dad moved over to that side to try to fix the problem. As he was doing that, the left side began to come off the wall again. Dad completely lost it. He tore all the wallpaper off the wall, crumpled it up, and threw it in the wastebasket. His language would have embarrassed a sailor. I stayed away!"

In one of my discussions with Terry, he teared up as he talked about the relationship he had with his father. Terry says, "I paid a big price for always thinking I was right, and Dad was wrong. The price I paid was giving up the love of my father and denying my father a son. That still bothers me today, even though Dad has passed on."

Years after his dad had passed, Terry wrote a letter to his father apologizing for denying him a son. "I hope he heard me, and I want my children to know and love me and to know I love them."

Wearing my psychologist's hat, I asked Terry to consider that no child has the responsibility for molding and shaping the parent-child relationship. That is the responsibility of the parent. I suggested that his father probably did the best he could with what he knew at the time and that the effects of living through the Great Depression had probably taken a huge toll on his emotional stability. I commended Terry for writing the letter to his father and counseled him to forgive himself in hopes that Terry could put his perceived guilt behind him.

Terry had a much closer relationship with his mom. "Mom served as a sort of smoke detector for me when it came to Dad's temper outbursts. She would warn me when Dad was angry, especially when he was angry with me."

In discussing his mom, Terry had this to say: "Mom liked to exaggerate the stories she told. For example, she led me to believe that my older brother owned a railway company. Dad, who would willingly tear down the castles she built in the sky, informed me that my brother was simply a clerk.

"Though Mom and Dad bickered constantly, I knew they loved each other: a testament to how opposites attract. Simple things, like Mom saying, 'You could have opened the door for me,' would trigger back-and-forth arguments. Mom would win most arguments. She was clearly better with words.

"I knew that Mom was very satisfied with her love life with Dad. One time I overheard Mom telling one of her friends how Dad would take her out in the tall grass and make love to her, taking a break from their work in the field. I also recall a ritual Mom and Dad had when they went to bed. The bickering disappeared and I could hear them softly talking to each other in loving tones. This was their together time and it gave us kids some comfort."

The middle school experience for Terry ended when he graduated fourth in his class of four students. He would pass into high school as he had all through middle school: on a conditional/social promotion basis.

Terry was not in the least bit excited about leaving his small Indiantown schoolhouse for the larger high school setting composed of mostly city kids.

Terry's high school years would prove to be tumultuous — and short-lived.

4

FARM BOY IN THE CITY

Terry entered St. Mary's High School in Saginaw, Michigan, as a ninth-grade student. Before entering, he had never even seen the school. It didn't take him long to discover he was a fish out of water: a poor student, a non-athlete, and completely out of sync with the dress codes of the city kids. His farmer boots, jeans, and leather jacket contrasted negatively with the khakis, pullover sweaters, and penny loafers that graced the halls and classrooms of St. Mary's.

Very soon after his first day at St. Mary's High School, Terry came home and found brand new clothing lying on his bed. To Terry's surprise, it matched the clothing the city kids were wearing at St. Mary's. Looking back, Terry figures his mom got a note from the school about his attire and therefore purchased appropriate clothing that clearly cost more than the family was used to spending. However, they didn't talk about it and the next day at school Terry was dressed like the other kids, conforming to what St. Mary's deemed appropriate. Unfortunately, his change in outside appearance was not accompanied with an internal change in his thinking.

In spite of his new clothing, Terry remained a misfit and hated every day he attended St. Mary's. His mechanical interests and skills were never tested and he failed most exams.

Wouldn't it be nice if Terry's parents got the following letter from the school principal:

Dear Parent,

Your child's examinations are about to start soon. I know you are really anxious for your child to do well. But please do remember: Among the students taking the exam there is

- *an artist who doesn't understand math.*
- *an entrepreneur who doesn't care about history.*

- *a musician whose chemistry marks won't matter.*
- *a sports person whose physical fitness is more important than physics.*
- *a dyslexic who can't read but has great mechanical skills and interests.*

If your child does get top marks, that's great. But if they don't, don't take away their self-confidence and dignity. For any student, one exam (or class) won't take away their dreams and talents. They are cut out for much bigger things in life. No matter what their score, you love them and do not judge them. And when you do this, watch them conquer the world. Please do not think that doctors and engineers are the only happy people in the world.
With warm regards,
The Principal

Misfits, like Terry, are expected to fit into a curriculum that does not meet their interests and talents. Perhaps it is the institutions that really need to change. What if schools and universities focused on unleashing the potential of each student by finding out what unique intelligences and passions drive them and then inspiring and nurturing the exploitation of those passions and talents?

Terry says, "I made one friend at St Mary's. He was a misfit like me. One day, I went to his house with him. He said, 'Please be sure to talk.' He knew that I was afraid to talk because I feared that what I said would come out all wrong."

Terry reveals, "I did learn some values at St. Mary's, such as 'Thou shalt not steal.' That didn't mean that I never would steal anything; it only caused me to feel ashamed when I did… Well, not always."

Terry's story reminded me about the boy who prayed to God for a bicycle. His mother told him, "God doesn't work that way," so he stole a bicycle and then asked God for forgiveness.

"I started dating a Saginaw High School student — let's call her Sue. Sue was a couple of years older than me and more than a bit on the wild side. She found joy in stealing things. I played the safer role of being her accomplice.

"Sue was bolder than me. For example, we

would both skip school and she would be the one to steal a bottle of wine from a local grocery store. We would get a buzz on. That buzz frequently triggered sexual arousal in me, and I was ready and willing to break any of my Catholic-upbringing values related to premarital sex with Sue. Just my luck, having sex (at least with me) wasn't a part of her game plan. Over time, that put a damper on, and eventually ended, our relationship."

Terry decided to transfer from St. Mary's to Arthur Hill Tech his sophomore year because it was a trade school that offered more classes that better matched Terry's mechanical interests and skills, such as drafting.

Things didn't work out as planned. Terry transferred to Saginaw High School after just one day of attendance at Arthur Hill Tech. According to Terry, "The moment I walked through the halls and realized the school had no girls, I left. I enrolled at Saginaw High School simply because it was a little closer to where I lived — and lots of girls went there.

"How does the song go, 'You've got to be a football hero to get along with the beautiful girls'? At Saginaw High I found out that was true. I wasn't a hero at anything. I was a benchwarmer in everything I tried. I got Ds and Es on my report card, and for skipping school I got suspended twelve times. The few kids who accepted me were just like me: not good in school and not interested in education in any way. We were interested in excitement and fast cars. Fast girls too — if we could find them."

At the end of his first semester at Saginaw High, Terry showed his very unimpressive report card to his parents. Their only comment was, "We thought you were going to Arthur Hill Tech." So much for parental involvement!

The farm work and his father were the factors which kept Terry's energies somewhat channeled. As Terry remembers, "Dad and I were never what you'd call close. The thing I remember most about him was that he was always mad and upset about something, usually about something I didn't do that I should have, or something I did do that I shouldn't have done. There were never any 'atta-boys' or pats on the back when I did something right.

"It wasn't in Dad's nature to give praise.

Yet, I always knew he respected me just by the responsibilities he trusted me with. I was doing a man's job on the farm and most of the guys I knew could not do that. The unwritten message I got from my dad was, 'Even if you can't read very well, you can always work hard.' Make no mistake though, my dad had no patience for sloppy work. No excuse was good enough for him. In some things, like farming, Dad had extremely high standards. Not something he discussed, of course. We never talked much at all.

"Yet, there was something there; something I didn't have a name for at that time. Today, I think of it as 'togetherness.' We spent a lot of time working together and I always wanted to please him, and even if he never said much until I did something wrong, it was enough to give me some satisfaction."

By the time Terry entered high school, the Duperon family was in better financial shape. Terry's dad showed his love for Terry when he bought him a 1955 Ford Sunliner convertible with a continental kit on the back. According to Terry, "The car, plus five dollars a week for gas — for me — that said it all."

Recently, Terry bought a restored 1955 Ford Sunliner convertible to add to his collection of classic cars. It was clearly an emotional, rather than a financial, investment. That car brings back a lot of memories.

When Terry was fifteen, he would go to the very popular teen dances held at the Saginaw Auditorium. The night usually began with the famous song "Honky Tonk" by The Bill Black Combo, and all the popular hits of the day followed. The famous local radio disc jockey was Ken Clark. Dance contests were the rage.

The 1960s were an exciting time for teens like Terry. Clothing styles were changing and the music scene was evolving, pretty much driven by the birth of rock 'n roll music. Fashion during these years featured a number of diverse trends. It was a decade that broke many fashion traditions, mirroring the dress codes of the popular bands and the music they played at that time. Blue jeans and black leather jackets were a teen trend that copied the dress style of Elvis Presley, and for a period of time, surf-rock styles took over, imitating California bands like the Beach Boys.

The television show *American Bandstand* taught young people the latest moves and new dance fads spread quickly.

- Fast partner dances: Swing dancing was still a hot dance trend in the 1950s, based on the jitterbug and swing moves of the big band era in the 1940s. Some swing dancers got quite fancy and acrobatic.
- Slow partner dances: There were many beautiful ballads played on the radio and at teen dances in the '50s and '60s. Young people capitalized on that.

- Group dances: Group dances were fun for a gang to do together. Perhaps the Stroll was the best known group dance of the day.
- Solo dances: Solo dances included the Chicken, the Twist, the Mashed Potato, and others.

All of the dance styles above captured the hearts and minds of teens and young adults who attended the dances and school functions, such as sock hops.

There were many rock 'n roll artists that prevailed in the '50s and '60s: Elvis Presley, Chuck Berry, Fats Domino, the Everly Brothers, Bill Haley and the Comets, Ray Charles, Buddy Holly, and Jerry Lee Lewis. These artists were soon joined by the Beatles, the Supremes, the Platters, and a host of others.

In Terry's hometown of Saginaw, Michigan, many dance champions emerged; to name just a few: Tommy Hammond, Karen Luplow, Bob Brandimore, Larry Keibler, and Loren Munn.

Lefty Frizzell's song "Saginaw, Michigan" topped the country music charts in 1964. Saginaw's Question Mark and the Mysterians topped the national charts with their hit single "96 Tears." Robert White's newly released book, *When the Kids Stopped Dancing,* highlights the local mid-Michigan bands that influenced the rise of rock 'n roll in the Great Lakes Bay Region. One of the featured bands was Don Steele and the Estyles.

Terry's goal at the dances was always to find a girl. Terry says, "I would look for a girl who would smile back at me. As I walked around the dance floor, I saw this pretty gal sitting on a guy's lap. Surprisingly, she smiled back at me. Game on!

"A while later I saw her standing on the side of the dance floor chatting with a friend of hers. I introduced myself and she told me her name was Jackie. She was a beautiful brunette with brown eyes and an alluring smile. Standing only four-feet-eleven-inches tall, she was built like a mini-model. I asked her to dance. After several dances, I asked her if she wanted me and my friend to give her a ride home. Without hesitation, she said, 'Sure. Why not?'

"Our driver parked the car at Ojibway Island. We necked in the back seat. Maybe a little light petting, but no sex. Not that night. But that would soon change, due to the convenience of having the backseat of my 1955 Ford Fairlane Sunliner convertible I got on my sixteenth birthday.

"Jackie was a real pretty gal. Besides that, she was also smart in school and confident enough that when things didn't go her way, she would let people know."

Terry remembers that he was frequently in trouble during those teen years. "When I was sixteen, I went to a neighborhood graduation party where the beer was flowing freely. I was drinking more than my share. In spite of my lack of sobriety, I decided to go out and get some more beer. I knew I could get it from a bar that was willing to sell to minors like me.

"My car had glasspack mufflers that made a cool, sort of angry, growling sound. Dad could hear my car pulling out of the neighbor's drive and he knew that I had been drinking. When I didn't come home, he was angry. He immediately set out to find me and get me back home. He obviously thought I would be heading for one of the drive-in restaurants like the State Drive-In, the Strand Drive-In, or Richie's Drive-In, where us teens tended to hang out." On Terry's way home, he got stopped by the police. Terry admits, "I was so drunk, I couldn't get my license out of my pocket when the cop asked for it. He took the beer I had purchased and sent me on my way."

Terry adds, "I got home before Dad did. Mom warned me as I walked through the door, 'Your dad is on the warpath about your drinking and driving, you better get to your room.' I did just that, but I could hear my dad yelling, 'What the hell is going on with these kids today? They drive around and around the drive-ins without ever stopping to buy a god-damn thing.'"

Terry pointed out to me that his mother reacted far differently than his dad did when Terry got into trouble, and it had a very different effect on Terry. For example, when he frequently got into trouble for skipping school more than he showed up, Terry remembered, "My skipping school never appeared to be much of an issue with my dad; he was far more concerned that I did my chores and worked the fields. Mom's reaction was to cry, and I couldn't take that. I felt that I was letting her down. I guess I knew in my heart that she had higher expectations for me than I had for myself."

Terry quit school in the eleventh grade. Then he decided to give it another try for about three months. Then he quit again. Why? Because Jackie gave him the startling news:

"I am pregnant!"

5

LONELY TOGETHER

The news that Jackie was pregnant shook Terry to his core. "I was dumbstruck, in a deep state of emptiness. Neither one of us knew what to do or where to turn. It was as if we had committed a high crime and now the world would know. The last thing I wanted was for my dad to find out. But, on the other hand, I could not very well let Jackie face things alone. We had to tell someone, so I confessed to her parents. It was as difficult as I imagined.

"Still, I couldn't bring myself to tell my own parents. It was only after Jackie's parents called them that it all came out. My folks were so hurt and Dad kicked into his Jackie Gleason mode. I had really let them down. After he calmed down a bit, he tried to talk to me about the pregnancy, but I wouldn't talk to him about it. Out of anger or frustration, Dad said to me, 'Who are you? Just like John?'"

His dad's statement cut Terry deeply because a little while earlier, Terry's brother-in-law John had run off with another woman, leaving Terry's sister alone with their children. They all moved in with Terry's parents. Later it was learned that John had burned up the engine of their car on the way to California, leaving Terry's dad with the additional problem of paying for a dead car. The last thing Terry wanted was for his dad to see him as irresponsible as he saw John.

Not wanting to talk to anyone close to him about the pregnancy, Terry turned to a priest for guidance. He was shocked at what the priest had to say. "He said I didn't need to marry Jackie. I could not believe my ears. At that moment, this Catholic boy became a confirmed atheist. There can't be a God if a priest gives that kind of advice."

While neither set of parents was thrilled about the union of Terry and Jackie, the norms at that time called for a marriage in this kind of circumstance. Therefore, the next move was to get married. Terry shares, "In June of 1961, when I was eighteen and Jackie was seventeen, we were married by a justice of the peace in what had to be the shortest ceremony on record. By that time, the ranting and raving were mostly over. We honeymooned for a week at my brother's cabin at Chain Lake in Hale, Michigan. I knew I wasn't really in love with Jackie and I knew she wasn't really in love with me.

"One day, several years later, while driving, I heard Ray Stevens sing the song 'Lonely Together.' I thought someone had written our honeymoon story and recorded it."

> *Every day it's easier to see*
> *That you're going to be a mother*
> *So here we are, honeymoon,*
> * hotel room*
> *Married to each other*
> *And the smile on your tender lips*
> * is brave*
> *But it don't cover up those tears*
> * you've cried*
> *And though I'm trying hard, all*
> * the emptiness I feel*
> *Is just too big to hide*
> *And we've got nothing in common*
> * but our name and our shame*
> *And the blame for letting passion's*
> * foolish flame burn wild*
> *And now we've got to cover up the*
> * fact with an act*

To atone for our mistakes and pro-
tect the child
But, baby, I think it's all in vain
We're not birds of a feather
Isn't it lonely together?

From interviewing Jackie's brother John about their years growing up together, it is easy to see that their childhood was not ideal. Many problems that would show up in Jackie's adulthood began in those early years at home with her parents.

Jackie and John's father came from a military background. He joined the Army Air Corps right out of high school where he was exposed to discipline and regimen as he rose to the level of being a bomber pilot with a rank of second lieutenant. He flew over thirty bombing missions. John remembers, "He would only talk about these missions when he was drunk. His time in the military was during WWII and he said he never flew a mission where his plane wasn't subjected to enemy fire. Once I asked Dad if he regretted killing Germans during the war and he said, 'Not any more than the Germans regretted killing my fellow soldiers.'

"As a bomber pilot, there was no room for poor planning or execution. This translated into the perfection Dad expected of Jackie and me. For example, if I cut the grass, the grass had to be evenly cut at six inches in length with straight rows. When I shoveled snow, I had to pass my dad's inspection."

John recalled that their mother could be charming and fun but she was also very judgmental and a poor housekeeper. "Mom would drink along with Dad a lot when we were young. Living in our household was very chaotic. Mom and Dad argued all day. Dad was what we call today 'a player.' He tended to wander — drinking too much and fooling around with other women. Mom was aware of this and it was a source of conflict and arguments. One time, he called from jail. He had been arrested for drunk driving in Ohio — and he was with another woman. The whole family went to bail him out. It was a very uncomfortable experience for all of us."

In her younger years, Jackie was very

feisty. As children, John remembers they would often physically fight, throwing blows, biting, and scratching each other. Jackie had their mother's good looks and their grandmother's fun and giving personality. She was very popular in school but she had trouble trying to keep up with her wealthier girlfriends.

John played football for Saginaw High School. He remembers that his parents never came to a single game, even though in one game alone he made twenty tackles. At the sports banquet, he was awarded the team's Most Valuable Defensive Player, while fellow teammate Jerry Patton was awarded the Most Valuable Offensive Player award. Neither his dad nor mom were there to see him be recognized by the coaches and the team.

Jackie's relationship to her mother was similar to John's relationship to his father. "I never got an 'atta-boy' and Jackie never received any praise or support either from Dad or Mom. For example, Jackie would get good grades, but would never get any praise for doing so. Like me, Jackie was never made to feel good enough. In addition, Mom never taught Jackie the things young growing girls should know. Mom and Dad never prepared us for life. They never talked to Jackie or me about the birds and the bees. We never witnessed affection, which is probably the reason why we both have had problems in sustaining relationships.

"In a nutshell, Dad and Mom taught us a lot of stuff by not teaching us a lot of stuff. They served as a good example of what *not* to be or do. Following in their footsteps, I find myself getting into no-win situations with my feelings, causing so many unnecessary breakups. I feel that Jackie suffered from the same issues."

———

After the honeymoon, Terry and Jackie moved into an upstairs bedroom at Terry's parents' home. Terry did not want to be a burden to his parents so after a couple of months, he found a place about a mile away from the Duperon's farm. The rental cost was twenty-five dollars a month. It had no running water, an outdoor toilet, and a small oil space heater to warm the house.

Tammy, age one, in 1963

Tammy, their first child, was born into that little house. One night in the weeks following her birth, the heater wasn't pushing out enough heat to warm the house. Terry rigged a blanket over the heater that created a tent, wrapped Tammy in another blanket, and placed her under the tent to ensure her warmth. During the night, Terry and Jackie took turns checking on the baby. The next day, Terry found an old wood-burning stove in his dad's garage. He hooked it up to the chimney, thus improving the heat situation.

The relationship between Terry and Jackie was also heating up, and not in a good way. Terry said, "Jackie's mother was a pain. She was very critical of me and of our living conditions. Once she brought a bag of groceries over to us. Then, she forever claimed she fed us through the winter." This frustrated Terry.

"Dad helped us out," Terry remembers. "Knowing the hard time we were having, he loaned me his truck so I could haul sugar beets at night. I believe he could have used the money himself, but it was his way of helping us out. The $1,800 I made hauling beets would have to carry us for a long time. We had to be extremely frugal."

After about a year and a half, Terry found another small house that had running water, indoor plumbing, and an oil space heater. Nothing fancy, but clearly a more comfortable living arrangement. As the first few years of their marriage passed, another baby, Terry, Jr., arrived.

Terry, Terry Jr., and Tammy

Terry Sr. did not miss attending school at all, but it was a different story for Jackie. Isolated from her friends and still just a teenager, her life consisted of changing diapers, cooking, and cleaning. She hated it and was not good at it.

Jackie's isolation would end when she aligned with two very different groups of friends. One group was made up of religious, family-type people. The other group was a wilder band of renegades — into drugs, alcohol, and sex. For a while, Jackie flip-flopped between these two groups; then she began to spend more and more time with her renegade friends.

Predictably, Jackie's behavior began to take a turn for the worse. "When I would get home from work," Terry recalled, "Jackie would take off and join her friends, leaving me or Tammy, our oldest, to tend to all of the childcare duties. By this time there were four younger siblings to Tammy: Terry Jr., Jeffrey, Laura, and Michael.

"Jackie spent more and more time away from me and the kids."

Life for Terry, Jackie, and the children was becoming more and more chaotic.

6

WHEN THE GOING GETS TOUGH

Tammy, Terry's oldest daughter, describes life in the Duperon household during that time as quite primitive. As I can now understand thinking of a mother of seventeen and a father of eighteen, they were kids raising kids. By the time Jackie had reached the age of twenty-four, they had five kids.

"Dad worked and was largely absent; Mom was at home and overwhelmed. Her behavior worsened. At our home in Bridgeport, I had to be about five years old and my brothers, Terry and Jeff, were ages three and two, respectively. We had a fenced-in backyard.

Mom would sometimes lock the three of us outside to play to gain some peace and take a nap. On one occasion, my brother Terry was running out the breezeway door and accidentally slammed his hands and then face into the glass door. All I heard was the loud noise, his crying, and then I saw his face full of blood. I began pounding on the door, screaming for Mom to come. Eventually, I was desperate and threw stones at the window. Mom, ready to raise heck, took one look at Terry and came running down.

"Our household was not easy. Given my Mom's upbringing and limited parental support, her mental health deteriorated as the demands of a young family grew. I once asked her, as an adult, what that time was like for her and she said it was a living hell.

"As a kid I would always hope Mom would get better and *this* was the time we were turning a corner. Mom would cycle in and out of better times and worse times. Yet, in the better times, I would always hope that *this was it*. I became pretty tough, pretty young, especially as the oldest, often finding comfort in caring for my siblings."

Terry reflects, "I had to place the kids with helpful relatives, because one day Jackie left to go stay with a friend in Detroit. It soon became evident that my relatives could not be a long-term solution. The kids were being separated from each other and I was stuck working long days to support Jackie and our children. This led me to make the tough decision of placing the children in the St. Vincent's Home in Saginaw." St. Vincent's Home provided orphans and indigenous children with food, shelter, education, and moral and religious training. It was founded in 1875 by Father Francis van der Bom, the first pastor at St. Mary's Church in Saginaw.

Tammy and Laura were placed in a room that had been cleared for them. As Laura and Tammy lay alone in single beds in a dorm that usually housed eight, Tammy remembers having the distinct thought, "Well, this looks like one more thing to go through." Michael was too young to stay overnight, so Terry picked him up daily after work.

During this time when the children were housed at St. Vincent's Home, Jackie was in Detroit, but eventually she came back from her friend's house and was admitted into a psychiatric ward at Saginaw General Hospital to undergo vigorous mental health treatment. She was drowning emotionally and this was an attempt to regain her well-being.

Tammy's recollections of St. Vincent's were generally positive. As the eldest, she responded well to the types of structure that existed there. "There was a pretty strict routine, and we weren't used to that. For example, when we got up in the morning, we had to make our bed, brush our teeth, and enter the breakfast room, all within about fifteen minutes. We had chores, scheduled meal times, and, much to my dismay, we had to eat everything on our plate. This was particularly a problem with peas, so I got pretty creative in how to get rid of them. Otherwise, we would have to sit there until done.

"I realized that there were some kids that had it worse. This was my first exposure to living with a diversity of personalities, family backgrounds, and nationalities. While I found our young nun leader, Sister Mary Lynn, was a gentle loving soul, I didn't quite know what to make of our housekeeper, Miss Katherine.

She was a short, large, and stern black woman who didn't take any guff from us girls. I was intimidated. I recall being 'called out' regarding my leadership. I had unknowingly influenced all the girls to be afraid of Miss Katherine. I had no idea that was what I was doing; I just thought her sternness was scary. However, Sister Mary Lynne had me consider how much Miss Katherine did for us, and how it must feel to have everyone afraid. I had not thought of that."

Tammy's younger siblings found St. Vincent's Home to be much more stressful than she did. They had a harder time adjusting to a schedule and to being subjected to close supervision.

Terry Jr. said, "I hated the time at St. Vincent's. The nuns there were very strict and they didn't know much about dealing with kids or the emotional aspects of us being there. The time was very stressful, which led me to throw up after meals, pee the bed, and generally be upset. It further upset me when Jeff was crying a lot and going through the same challenges I had."

Jeff said, "I hated the routine. It was so unlike what we were used to and the nuns treated us very harshly."

While at St. Vincent's, the Duperon kids enrolled in school. For Tammy, it was her first experience with a parochial school. The other children went to public school. They all felt underprepared for what to expect. That was very scary, especially for the young ones.

Laura said, "I was very scared when I went into school. Being the second youngest, none of my siblings or parents communicated with me on what to expect. I was going in blind."

Tammy adds, "We were at St. Vincent's for approximately nine months. When we came home to live with Dad, we all followed the structure we had become accustomed to at St. Vincent's. We made our beds, brushed our teeth, etc. This discipline did not last for very long."

In interviewing others who had spent time at St. Vincent's home, I found that their experience was much different from that of the Duperon children. In essence, it was much more positive. It was a safe haven for some children and youth, but clearly it was a personal experience for each child. Some loved it and others felt very differently. Since the Duperon children were not used to any structure in their lives, the adjustment for them was more difficult than it was for most children.

Terry says, "When Jackie eventually returned home, I thought, 'We can finally bring our kids home.' However, Jackie was not ready for the kids to come home because, during her time in the psychiatric ward, she had become addicted to different medications. She started to get prescribed drugs from multiple doctors. She was able to do this because she was smart, attractive, and could talk her way through anything."

Tammy recalls what it was like when she and her siblings were eventually allowed to return home from St. Vincent's: "Mom's escape was sleep. I remember at one point, when she would be so stoned and painfully irrational, my mom simply imploded and it was terrifying." Terry adds, "Jackie was constantly ridiculing the children and on some occasions actually became physical."

Due to witnessing her mom's behavior, Tammy explains, "I swore that I would never be a person without a strong sense of 'self.' This led to me investing in a lifetime of personal growth and development classes, therapy, and extensive study of Landmark Education and other platforms." These things helped Tammy overcome childhood trauma and identity issues, and move on to a satisfying personal life and productive business career.

"As kids, our behavior was challenging to say the least. While I tried to help my younger siblings with projects like building a fort, or directing a play, things would sometimes become violent and explosive. This required me to manhandle the kids to try to get things under control.

"I remember never quite knowing what we would face coming home. It was utterly unpredictable. Dad talked about the fact that if Mom was up in the morning, the uproar would become so great that we would cry as we walked to the bus. All I know is that I became very good at turning off whatever was going on at home as I left for school.

"I recall being in ninth grade with an amazing young teacher, Mr. Davis, who, as a former EMT, taught biology and a year-long first aid course. In one of his classes, we discussed suicide and how we could call an ambulance and have someone admitted if someone were a danger to themselves or others. I found this to be a whole new possibility for getting Mom help. I was having to constantly check on her to see if she was still breathing because of the level of medication she used. I went home that day and found Mom drugged. I warned her and said, 'Mom, if you do this again, I will be calling an ambulance.' She did it again so I called.

"It was a scene I will never forget, as she fought those who came. She was in cardiac ICU for three days. It was nowhere near the worst incident and was an eye opener to how close to death Mom was. I took a one-gallon bag of drugs to her doctor. He was appalled. He had no idea that other doctors were also prescribing."

7

THE NEXT CLEAR STEP: DIVORCE

In Terry's marriage, things were getting worse each day. Terry says, "I would be working twelve hours a day. I know now that I was a part of the problem in our marriage. I didn't know how to cope with all of the chaos she caused me and the family. I would argue with Jackie, or withdraw. I probably could have played a bigger and better role as a father, but coming home was emotionally exhausting. Most nights when I got home from work, Jackie would leave and join her friends to enjoy the wilder side of her life. At the time, this really bothered me, but as I look back, I could have done more to help the children cope."

It is said that we are always one piece of information away from understanding. Terry and Jackie were two young kids thrown into marriage and parenthood; it was not a formula for success. What Terry didn't know until toward the end of their marriage was that Jackie had been diagnosed with a mental health condition called Borderline Personality Disorder (commonly referred to as BPD). Simply stated, BPD is hard to diagnose, and even harder to treat. The main features of BPD are:

- a pervasive pattern of instability of mood in interacting with others and in controlling their emotions.
- black and white thinking (generally referred to as splitting).
- idealization and devaluation episodes.
- chaotic interpersonal relationships, self-image, identity, and behavior.

- disturbances in the individual's sense of self.

People with BPD are also typically very impulsive. The person's emotions may often be characterized as being unstable and unpredictable. Jackie manifested these behaviors as a pattern in their marriage.

BPD is more prevalent in females (75 percent). BPD affects only about 2 percent of the general population. If a person has BPD, the risk is slightly increased for it to be passed down to one's children.

Most people with BPD, like Jackie, do not seek out treatment until the disorder has started to significantly interfere with or otherwise impact the person's behavior, or coping resources are stretched too thin to deal with stress or other life events.

According to the National Institute of Mental Health, mental health issues are common in the United States. Nearly one in five adults in America lives with a mental illness (51.5 million in 2019). The impact on families ranges from mild to severe.

What I say about BPD is meant to be explanative and to bring compassion to a very difficult path for humans to navigate. It is not meant to dismiss all or even some of Jackie's behaviors, both self-destructive and destructive toward others. It is intended to shed light on how little control Jackie had over her thoughts and behaviors when in the midst of her illness and her addiction. It is the nature of humans to want to label something to help make it simple to understand. It is more important to remember that a whole human being lives inside these labels and this person is capable of finding moments of love, connection, and contribution *in spite* of his/her condition. Jackie was a human coping with and compensating for the difficult life she lived as a child (as her parents had lived before her). It is possible to view her behaviors as methods of coping and survival. However, they did come with great costs to all affected by them.

There is a general honeymoon period for BPD-affected people in a relationship, followed by recognition that the partner is not faultless. Splitting (black and white thinking) sets in, quickly moving the BPD person's perception from idealization to devaluation (for example, quickly moving from "I love you" to "I hate you," or "This is a great life" to "This is a horrible life"). BPD relationships are, in a word, stormy! It is not uncommon to experience a great deal of turmoil and dysfunction.

For example, there was a letter that Terry revealed from 1973 that was in a card given to him for Father's Day in a time when Jackie was in one of her more upbeat moods. In it we find her heart for her children, for her husband, and feeling the blessings of her life. Jackie often sought healing and solace in a spiritual connection at these times. Her gift was to give thanks for the father that he was, a prayer for his blessings by his Savior, honoring that God chose him to be her husband and blessed them with their children. These times of temporary respite were offset with difficult, hurtful, and sometimes volatile incidents and periods. The letter states:

> *Dearest Terry and earthly father of our children,*
> *My gift to you today is nothing visible, but it's the unseen riches that are most important*

(although they are seen, for we reflect them by the look on our faces, the way we speak and act with others).

A very special prayer goes up today for you that our Very Special Precious Savior, Jesus, will draw you nearer to himself and bless you with his wisdom, love, peace, joy, and knowledge.

Also, a special prayer of thanksgiving goes up today to our Heavenly Father, who in His infinite wisdom, chose you to be my husband and the kid's earthly father. We thank Him for this blessing.

Jackie

When the kids were fairly young, "Jackie's behavior had become more and more erratic," remembers Terry. "She had no peace with me, with the kids, or within herself. I blamed her behavior on her having psychological problems. Because I had medical insurance through [my job at the time], I was able to take her to see a psychiatrist. He prescribed drugs that he believed would help her and, for a short while, they did.

"Then Jackie began going to different doctors to get more prescriptions — legally and illegally. Clearly, she was addicted. I didn't really understand addiction at that time, nor did I fully realize what Jackie's addiction was doing to me and the kids. The situation kept worsening."

Terry experienced mood shifts with a great deal of frequency throughout this period of indecision. He began to feel unlovable and blamed Jackie for much of what was going on. He couldn't see any future with Jackie but he also couldn't see a future without her. This allowed the marriage to drift for many years.

"Jackie was out some nights until four in the morning. Her friends were telling me she was having affairs and I would lay awake, my thoughts shifting back and forth between anger and worry ('Am I in love with her? Do I hate her?'), then ponder, 'Am I going crazy?'"

It appears that Gene Watson nailed what Terry was going through when he recorded the song "It's Crazy When a Man Can't Get a Woman Off His Mind."

I've been fighting with these sheets

*again, can't make myself lie
    still
My pillowcase is soaking wet and
    yet I feel a chill
It takes all that I can do these
    days to just survive the nights
It gets crazy when a man can't get
    a woman off his mind
When a man can't shake a memory, he runs hot and cold and
    blind
He hates her, then he loves her,
    then he hates her one
    more time
Your love has such a grip on me, it
    chokes me like a vine
It gets crazy when a man can't get
    a woman off his mind*

The years leading up to Terry's divorce from Jackie were hard on everybody. When I interviewed Laura, Terry's youngest daughter with Jackie, she said, "Mom was not present much of the time, and was frequently drugged. She was not capable of being a mother. Like *Lord of the Flies*, we raised ourselves. I did grow to feel quite capable and now I feel like I can manage almost any challenge."

Terry remembers, "Six months before I decided to end my marriage, I had met this attractive twenty-three-year-old woman I will call Beckie. She made me feel lovable again. Feeling lovable gave me a strength I had lost. I knew what I was doing with Beckie was wrong, but it was what I needed at the time. It was the only time I was unfaithful while I was married to Jackie. This affair had nothing to do with love. She liked being with me and we were having fun. Neither of us saw or wanted a future for this relationship."

Terry reflects, "I was beginning to feel I could possibly have a better life without Jackie: I could love and be loved by someone." Terry's affair with Beckie was a pivotal point in Terry's life. He finally saw new possibilities for a more fulfilling life moving forward.

"The divorce turned out to be a no-fault divorce so I needed to prove that I was the better parent. First, I got temporary custody of the kids. The Friend of the Court office said, 'I don't think you can care for the kids.' So, I had three years to prove my parental capabilities."

Tammy says, "By the time I was fifteen, Dad decided to file for divorce. There was very little chance those days for a man to win custody of the kids. The months leading up to the finalization of the divorce were excruciating. I was not only afraid for my mom, but it was hard watching Dad go through the pain. When we were children, we went to see the Friend of the Court. Each of us claimed, 'It would probably be better if we went with Dad.' I couldn't be disloyal to Mom and say I preferred it, although I did in a roundabout way."

Terry says, "I was afraid of losing my kids in the divorce, but because I felt a new sense of strength, I decided to go for it. I met with a judge who gave me thirteen things to consider. I got people to vouch for me. I took the kids to church every Sunday and spent time with them. As the kids became teenagers, I felt I had to separate them from Jackie. An incident with one of the kids striking back became the last straw for me. I knew at that moment the kids' respect for Jackie and her authority was almost completely lost. This could not go on, for all of us."

In Tammy's own words, "I ran the house by the time the divorce was filed. I felt safer if I could make sure everyone had the things they needed. I was driven to achieve. Yet, after the divorce, I noticed that I felt like crying all the time. I finally asked Dad if I could talk to someone. I saw Dr. Norman Westlund, the director of the Child Guidance Clinic in Saginaw. With all these overwhelming feelings, I wanted to be sure that I was not following Mom's footsteps. He assured me that what I was experiencing was typical for children after divorce and that helped me move forward."

While Tammy was getting emotional guidance, Terry was focusing on moving up in the world of business in hopes of fulfilling his dream of becoming an inventor.

8
CLIMBING THE CAREER LADDER

Terry had faced serious challenges with employment. "I had been a misfit in school, and I knew my school credentials wouldn't fly with potential employers. I couldn't even fill out applications or read manuals. Would I be a misfit in the work world as well?

"On the brighter side, I had proven to myself that I had a dream and mechanical abilities. Also, Dad's role-modeling of a strong work ethic prepared me to do the same. I was a farm boy, and farmers have an attitude that, whatever problem or situation arises, you must deal with it. There is never an escape hatch."

Early on, when Terry got the news of Jackie's first pregnancy, he started to move from job to job, finding opportunities by presenting himself as a little more qualified than he really was, and then by working really hard to learn what he needed while doing the work. For example, since he couldn't read, he managed to get others to fill out his applications, and since he couldn't read manuals, he would apply what he had learned on the farm about tearing down machines and equipment and then putting them back together. Drawing on his farm work with his dad, he knew he had the ability to visualize how machines ran and to accurately diagnose problems that others were not able to see.

Terry's inability to read and write beyond about the third-grade level would be a serious barrier to success. However, Terry was determined to use whatever talents and skills he did have to earn a decent living. He had no choice except, as he says, "to go with what I've got and not to worry about what I'm not!"

He would keep his inability to read and write a secret. Terry would use his mechanical skills and street smarts rather than what he had learned in school. He knew the application process would be a stumbling block as he tried to get jobs for which he really didn't qualify.

Terry's life on the farm had been his real life. His dream of becoming an inventor, and living the lifestyle that that dream would make possible, kept its legs as a result of his unfaltering efforts to apply his skills to fixing things. That dream, set in the mind of a third-grader, was ever present in the recesses of Terry's mind.

Because inventors and explorers were Terry's heroes as a child, he had enjoyed building igloos in the winter and forts in the summer. He had developed the ability to visualize how to make things work. He would design the end product in his mind, then put it on paper, and then build the product. This pattern would be the cornerstone of any future job or career success.

Terry says, "I left my first job at a junkyard

for a job at Sears in the mechanics area, changing tires and installing mufflers. This was a much better job, but the pay was low. I don't really know why, but the boss simply walked up to me one day and said, 'You're fired!'

"I was lucky to land a job working at Rubin Schultz Construction in Saginaw, Michigan. Rubin was an old military veteran. I got this job by accident. I was going to apply for a mechanic's job at another place. By mistake, I stopped at Rubin Schultz's contracting business and found out I was at the wrong place. However, when I told him I was going to apply for a truck mechanic's job, he looked at me and said, 'I need one of those.'" Terry was hired on the spot.

"Rubin had a poorly running flatbed truck. I figured out that it was a linkage problem and I got it running like a top."

Rubin asked, "What did you do to fix my truck?" Terry was about to explain, but then, "the old mechanic stepped in front of me and took full credit for fixing the truck. I couldn't believe a guy would ever do that. It really shocked me. I probably didn't protest because of the years I spent never challenging the authority of my dad. Old habits die hard." Terry left Rubin's after putting in about a year of service.

B&K Tool and Die

In 1961, Terry's cousin, Barney Poineau, called him one day to tell him that B&K Tool and Die was looking for someone to steam clean parts. B&K Tool and Die was located in Bridgeport, Michigan. Tool makers at B&K constructed precision tools or metal forms, called dies, that were used to cut, shape, and form metal and other materials. They also made metal molds for die casting and for unmolding plastics, ceramics, and composite materials. Terry says, "The B and K stood for the partners, named Becker and Kostrzewa. There were two Bs and two Ks: Julius Becker and Steve Bugai, and Joe and Val Kostrzewa. I learned that B&K liked to hire farmers and military vets because of their work ethic."

B&K had a policy that prohibited hiring

relatives, but Terry slipped under the radar. Terry was hired. His first job was cleaning parts. According to Terry, "I fit that farmer mold and was happy to work ten- to twelve-hour shifts because of the overtime pay. Sometimes I got to work seven days per week. Looking back on this now, I realize I had left the kids to fend for themselves against Jackie's erratic behavior. Back then, I thought I was doing the best for them by bringing in the money since Jackie didn't work.

"When I ran out of parts to clean, I began working with the journeymen, a group of tough WWII veterans. They treated me harshly — at first. Once when I was holding one end of a pipe in place for one of these guys, he looked at me and sternly said, 'I could replace you with a C-clamp!'

"But these fellow journeymen were teaching me the trade. I just had to put up with all of their guff. After having worked for so many years for my dad, putting up with their harassment was a cakewalk. I was never a very good craftsman because I couldn't read the required manuals, so I created other ways to do things. I kept redesigning processes so that I could do them. To show the boss how my process worked, I asked him to give me two weeks to completely tear down a machine and put it back together again in working order. He agreed to let me do that, not really understanding why I wanted to. I had learned on our farm to do that kind of tearing apart and reassembling machines (like lawn mowers that didn't require manuals) and I figured I could best do my job if I followed my own pattern of thinking and doing things. This process also gave me a way of knowing what inventory was needed.

"The experience working for my demanding father would serve me well because I learned to do what I needed to without reading a book of directions." Terry had learned to accept criticism in a mood of inquiry rather than a mood of resentment. He created a system that allowed him to do machine rebuilds in a much shorter period of time than the others could do it.

"Initially, my fellow journeymen criticized me. Then they began to use the new processes I had invented. They would simply watch what I was doing and then repeat the processes I had created to save time. Because my new process was so fast, B&K gave me five machines. I took more time tearing the machines down, but I spent less time putting them back together again. I like simplicity of design and uncomplicated operations."

Perhaps best of all, Terry created a system for keeping track of parts. In combination with Terry's tear-apart-and-reassemble process combined with the systematic parts/retrieval inventory system, B&K was able to do rebuilds much faster.

Those same journeymen who treated Terry so harshly in the beginning had grown to respect Terry's work ethic and his creative understanding of how to maintain, rebuild, and repair machines. What was once a one man, one machine norm was suddenly outmoded by Terry's new method.

"As my job performance improved, B&K put me on the road to set up, service, and rebuild complicated machines. I had to understand hydraulics, pneumatics, mechanics, and more." This was a great opportunity, but Terry almost let his fear of not being able to fill out the necessary forms to enter a client's plant get the best of him.

"I threw up twice on my way to my first service call. I was so nervous about not being able to get into the factory because I couldn't read or write. So, I faked a hand injury. I said to the gatekeeper, 'Can you fill this form out for me?' She said 'Sure,' and I was in. When I looked at the first machine, I was surrounded by a team of engineers. I was beyond nervous. I stood there almost frozen in place. I couldn't even find the green starting switch on the machine.

"Fortunately, I settled down. It did not take long for the engineers to like me. It helped that I had an expense account for the first time in my life, and I was able to buy their lunches. That felt good and got the engineers to respect me and my work."

Terry left B&K Tool and Die in 1967 when a new opportunity arose, but his time and experience at B&K was a life-changer in many ways. He proved to himself that he could perform up to and sometimes beyond the expectations of his boss and his fellow workers. His steady income enabled him to buy his first home at a cost of eight thousand dollars. And it was at B&K that Terry was allowed to explore and design. His talents were beginning to be recognized and the supervisor on the assembly floor gave Terry permission to follow his instincts.

It was during this time at B&K that Terry was credited with his first patent for a drill motor that could get relative square nuts out of a hand-drilled hole. According to Terry, "When I opened my letter, it read:

'United States Patent Office:
Terry Duperon, Inventor'

"My thoughts drifted back [to my childhood]. I got very emotional. I actually cried, thinking about that little dyslexic third-grader committing to becoming an inventor. I could feel the same emotions as I did back then."

Wilson Engineering

Terry next got a job as a draftsman at Wilson Engineering in a very fascinating way. He met a gentleman named Don Lefave, chief engineer at Wilson Engineering, located in Saginaw, Michigan. Terry and Don were enjoying a beverage at the bar in the MBS Airport in Freeland, Michigan. In their casual conversation, Don mentioned that Wilson had posted a job opening for a draftsman. Terry told Don he was very interested.

Terry had never drawn anything, but he could read blueprints and understood mechanical devices. Once again, Terry never let himself be the one to limit himself.

In Terry's words, "I took the job at Wilson Engineering at one-half the pay I was receiving at B&K. Why would I do this? I knew I could copy or redraw, but I could not create drawings from scratch. I had to copy the words, words like concentric, to get away from the spelling. *I wanted to learn how to draw.*

"The boss looked at my first drawing, and put red marks through the whole thing. This happened several times. Slowly, I figured it out."

Eventually, Terry decided to leave Wilson Engineering. "When Wilson's sales slowed down, they began downsizing. I was building a house in Indiantown at the time and the pay at Wilson Engineering would not be enough to cover the costs of my house. My only two options were to either sell the house after building, or find a new job. So, I began to look for a new opportunity."

KLC

"I landed a new job at KLC, a startup company. I was very slow at drafting but the engineers at KLC saved my job by pointing out the fact that I was helping them by finding their mistakes. I could do this because I knew how all the parts were made. I gained this knowledge from serving that apprenticeship at B&K.

"Drawing on my farm equipment experience, I was good at seeing why things wouldn't work. For example, an engineer showed me a device they were using to put in the soft plugs, and I said, 'It's not going to work. When you start the machine, it will spit plugs all over the room.' And that's exactly what happened."

Terry applied for a sales position within KLC, and he got it. But he ran into a problem when his boss insulted his new customers.

After touring the facility, his boss said, "This place is so filthy that I will never drink your beer again." Terry protested, defending his client. Soon thereafter, Terry was fired in 1971.

Trippensee

One of Terry's clients while he had been working for KLC had been Trippensee Corporation in Saginaw, Michigan. This company made teaching aids and did core and water samples. "I got a lucky break. When I applied for this job, they assumed I was an engineer because I had been selling engineering services. So, I never told them that I wasn't. They offered me a job as their sole engineer and as assistant to the president. I took projects home to design."

Terry discovered a problem with one of the core catchers while at Trippensee. The core catchers went into the mud or sand in the bottom of a body of water and took a sample. Customers were frustrated by the fact that the cores were coming out distorted and would not stay in the catcher while the sample was being retrieved. There was nothing on the market that solved this problem, so Terry designed a way to fix it. This Eggshell Core Catcher became another patent of Terry's. He received multiple patents while at Trippensee, until he left the company in 1975 for an opportunity of his own making.

9

A PROFOUND TRANSFORMATION

God promises a safe landing, not a calm passage. If God brings you to it, He will bring you through it!

— author unknown

In this chapter we digress to discuss a profound transformation that changed Terry's work, family, and spiritual life. The seed for this transformation was planted during a time when Terry attended Al-Anon meetings with his coworker, Bob Premo. Bob

Premo had befriended Terry while working at B&K Tool and Die. He noticed that Terry was struggling. Upon learning what Terry was going through at home, with Jackie's addiction and his hectic home life, Bob suggested that Terry join him in attending an Al-Anon meeting to gain some mutual support from people whose lives have been affected by someone else's drinking. Bob was a recovering alcoholic whose own thinking had been influenced by immersion in the twelve-step personal inventory espoused by AA and Al-Anon.

Terry says, "I was very reluctant to attend the Al-Anon meetings at first, but I was at my wits' end. I knew I had to do something." The meeting was held at a rented hall. Terry recalls, "All of us sat around a table and introduced ourselves, using first names only. For a moment, I thought about sneaking out the side door, but there wasn't one."

Attendance at weekly Al-Anon meetings with Bob helped Terry see value in this sort of personal inventory — looking inward to gain better insights. Bob confronted Terry with the observation that he often spoke of "Jackie's problems" or with blame for Jackie, but didn't often take responsibility for any of his portion of blame. Many things that he had done, such as being an absent father, had put a heavier burden on Jackie. Terry became more introspective and more self-aware. He started living a more thoughtful life.

Bob Premo and Terry Duperon

Terry learned that the first step toward coping with living with an alcoholic (or anyone with other addictions) is to affirm a belief in a higher power who is waiting on call. For years, Terry had been living as an atheist, so the slow process of returning to a belief in God represented a profound transformation that would continue to transpire over the years.

As he attended the weekly meetings and moved through the twelve steps, he grappled with the self-inventory process that required Terry to engage in a fearless moral inventory. Terry took a hard look at himself and, as he says, "I did not like what I saw — not even a little bit."

Terry became determined to change his life and the lives of his children for the better. He took on an entirely new role as a present and involved parent, and with it came a new outlook and a new hope for a better future. He knew that this hope came from his return to a belief in God. "I did not see God as a fortune teller, as I had earlier in life. I just knew He was with me. I became strongly committed to becoming a better version of myself."

There was one specific occurrence that powerfully influenced Terry's transformation. After one of the Al-Anon meetings, an elderly lady observed that Terry was really struggling with how to handle his family situation. She looked directly into Terry's eyes and softly said, "Ask God to come into your life! Do this, while you are lying in bed, before you go to sleep."

With some skepticism, that night Terry followed the elderly lady's advice. Terry remembered it as "no bolt of lightning, no nothing." Yet slowly but surely, he had come to trust that he had spiritual guidance, and that he was not alone as he navigated his way through the rough waters of life.

Terry has reflected on how his belief in God influenced his thoughts and behaviors. "I began to address each challenge or opportunity that was presented to me with a new sense of confidence." He started by asking himself these questions:

- Knowing who I am by the things I love and care about, the people and things that matter to me, does

this opportunity move me closer to, or further away from, the man God created me to be?
- Does this opportunity take me closer or further away from the dream I envision for my life?

Terry's profound transformation took him from atheism to a belief in a higher power and Terry surrendered. "Coming from this place, I simply take the first clear step and then another, ever forward to some place that moves me closer to my dream of living the life I love. This is what I call *living in inquiry*: I seek out the next clear step toward the fulfillment of my dream. As I look back, I can see that each step I have taken was a choice: to go left, to go right, to go forward, or even to not go at all."

As time passed, Terry began to get a better grasp of the impact his profound transformation was having on his life. Up to this point in Terry's adult life, when things went wrong, he got weaker and lost confidence. While he had been living as an atheist, every setback put Terry into a downward spiral. This took Terry's emotions through feelings of worthlessness to hopelessness to hostility and finally, to isolation — *"I am alone and no one can help me."*

After he invited God into his life, he eventually began to reverse this downward spiral. His belief in God triggered the feeling that he was not alone in his quest to deal with the challenges in his life, and it changed his approach to achieving happiness and joy. Now he had a new sense of gratitude and he realized he was trusting in the guidance of God. Even when things got harder, he met each challenge and set-back with a new confidence. He still faces serious challenges, but he faces his problems differently — somehow knowing that with God's help, he can be less anxious mentally and more spiritually attuned. As Terry says, "Nothing defeats me."

As Terry looks back, he fully realizes that it was this profound transformation from atheism to believing in a higher power that first ignited his enduring belief that *nothing will defeat me and I will never be the one to hold me back!*

There had been no bolt of lightning at that earlier time when he lay in bed asking God to join him in his quest. What did happen to him was an incremental awakening to how significantly his life had changed from easily entering into a downward spiral with every setback to truly believing that nothing could defeat him.

It was at this time when Terry began to more fully expand his commitment to living in inquiry. He positioned himself to attend a multitude of religious ceremonies, looking for commonality and differences in beliefs, attitudes, and expectations. He also chose to stop looking into the faults of other people. Terry began to look closely at the life of Christ, and he discovered that Jesus Christ modeled all that is good about humanity.

Years later, when Terry financially and emotionally hit rock bottom, he saw what he calls glimpses of God's grace, which fed his soul. It was 1980 and Terry was only thirty-seven years old when he began to feel chest pain — it wasn't pulsating pain, it was just a steady pain that kept getting worse. First he tried to go to bed to see if the pain would go away, but it kept getting more and more intense. Then he was driven to the hospital where it was quickly discovered that he was having a heart attack. He was placed in intensive care. According to Terry, "I began to pray, asking, 'What is going to happen to me?' I realized even in that condition that God is not a fortune teller, but that he is always with me."

The doctors administered morphine — no more pain, no more prayers.

Things went from bad to worse when Terry flatlined twice. The first flatline was caused by the drugs that Terry was given to thin his blood. His chest filled up with blood. The second flatline was caused when they gave Terry a drug to slow his heart rate down. Terry's heart rate stopped.

According to Terry, "I awoke to find Dr. Roger Kahn pushing a pacemaker into my chest without numbing it. I could feel the pain of what he was doing. When I saw Dr. Kahn, I knew I wasn't in heaven.

"After I had experienced all of this, I was so weak I had to hug the curtain to get to the toilet. I was so depressed at home for three days, I spent most of my time crying on the couch."

As Terry became stronger, he started walking to the end of the driveway. Once he got comfortable with that, he extended his walk to a mile, and then he started running to work every day, roughly a six-mile run.

Terry survived the heart attack and began to take his life more seriously: he quit smoking and caffeine entirely, and limited his drinking to very moderate amounts. "I asked God for his help. I did not and do not believe God to be a fortune teller; I just wanted him to walk through this life with me and help me break free of the shackles and anxieties that were holding me back from fulfilling my dream."

Terry's book, *Glimpses of God's Grace*, reveals how positive changes were triggered by thoughts that showed him the way when he most needed guidance on his journey.

Psychologist Martin Seligman has done many studies on the pursuit of happiness. In his book *Authentic Happiness*, he defines three paths to happiness:

1. Pleasure: An individual leading a life of pleasure can be seen as maximizing positive emotions and minimizing negative emotions.

2. Engagement: An individual living a life of engagement constantly seeks out activities that allow him or her to be in a flow. Flow, coined by Mihaly Csikszentmihalyi, is a state of deep, effortless involvement. It occurs when we concentrate our individual attention on activities that are moderately challenging to us. When you are in flow, it may seem that your sense of self vanishes and time slows. To achieve flow, you must identify your signature strengths (that is, strengths that are deeply characteristic of yourself) and learn how to practice them.
3. Meaning: An individual living a life of meaning belongs to and serves something bigger than himself. These larger entities could be such things as religion, country, or ideas.

It is important to note that the three happiness orientations are not equal. Orientations to engagement and meaning are much more predictive of life satisfaction compared to the orientation to pleasure.

Years later, Seligman added two more orientations to happiness and coined the acronym PERMA:

1. Pleasure
2. Engagement
3. Relationships
4. Meaning
5. Accomlishment

Terry intuitively began to move through the PERMA orientations to happiness offered by Seligman. After his profound transformation from atheism to a believer, Terry began trying to lead a more fulfilling life. He began to experience more positive emotions, he found pleasure from engaging with his children, and created a better balance between home life and work life. He also began to experience more gratitude as he exercised his signature strengths. Terry's dream gave his life meaning, and then his accomplishments followed. He started feeling stronger and more resilient. He had a new sense of bounce-back-ability.

Terry no longer asks God for things. He simply feels that God is present within him and will guide his choices. Terry decided he would only act on what is clear as a first step and see where it took him. Then he would wait for what appears as the second step. He would never ask for two steps at a time.

Terry surrendered his life to God. He points out, "Whatever we surrender to becomes our master. If we surrender to drugs, alcohol, sex, or money — that is now our master."

Terry's transformation moved to a higher plane years later during a period of time when he served as president of the Serra Club. The Serra Club is a Catholic organization for men and women from all walks of life, all dedicated to promoting and fostering vocations.

One of the guest speakers for the club was Sister Laurene. Sister Laurene was a Roman Catholic nun who had spent forty years of her life in the cloistered community of a convent, protected from contact with the outside world and dedicated to silent prayer.

At the club she gave a speech that was movingly spiritual in nature, and it profoundly touched Terry's heart. Terry says, "There was something God-like about her presence that I can't describe, but she had something I really wanted. When you were with Sister, it was as if she was fully and completely present — present in a way that 'she' disappeared. I imagined that was what Jesus was like. No ego. After her speech, I told her that." Her response was, "Come and see me and we'll talk."

Sister Laurene during her last visit with Terry one month before her death while in hospice care.

That initial meeting

led to frequent meetings that had a big impact on Terry's life. Her empathetic listening allowed Terry to verbalize what he was thinking. This helped Terry mourn his losses. It also freed him of anxieties and enabled him to begin to feel good about himself during challenging times. Her reaffirming advice was, "Surrender to God."

Terry saw Sister Laurene as a sort of conduit to God. Whenever he felt the need, he would meet with Sister. Toward the end of her life, she said to Terry, "Now I want what you've got. I get lonely, so please come and visit me." Sister Laurene passed away peacefully in her sleep at the age of ninety-two.

10

TERRY ENTERS THE ENTREPRENEURIAL WORLD

Prior to sharing Terry's entry into the entrepreneurial world, I believe it is useful to provide some context that helps one grasp the risks and rewards of engaging in an entrepreneurial venture which can be characterized by the taking of financial risks in the hope of profit. An entrepreneurial spirit thrives on meeting the next challenge.

Risks

All too often, once on their path, entrepreneurs face what researchers refer to as *the boom and bust cycle*. That cycle refers to periods during which a business expands and contracts. In general, entrepreneurial economic forecasts aren't perfectly reliable. Neither, of course, are the hunches and intuitions of entrepreneurs.

Entrepreneurs tend to take on unnecessary expenses when times are good, but this can sink them when sales and profits slow down. In particular, entrepreneurs tend not to be wary of paying higher recurring expenses, such as rent. They need to pay continuing attention to the following examples of unnecessary expenses when times are good:

- extravagant expense accounts.
- over-reliance on high-priced professional advisors.
- products that are too expensive or don't carry their weight.
- marginal customers you'd be better off without.

The above offered list is, of course, not exhaustive. Trimming costs when times are good helps your profits, and makes a difference between success and failure when the cycle turns downward.

Entrepreneurs also must think twice before adding expenses that may be hard to cut, or even cost more to cut than they do to keep. Chief among these costs is people. It can be painful to lay off workers in the event of an economic downturn, and the costs for severance pay, unemployment insurance, outplacement, and re-training can be steep.

Rewards

It is clear that the entrepreneurial world has its risks. But, like all things in this binary world we live in, it also has its rewards. To fully realize the rewards of this domain you must be willing and able to live with ambiguity and risk.

Most people prefer the certainty of a steady paycheck. The flip side is that the rewards of entrepreneurship are massive. For example, 80 percent of millionaires in America are entrepreneurs. Other rewards include such things as a flexible schedule, autonomy, creating a career that aligns with your values, constant growth, and more.

Once you commit to this lifestyle, you can start building financial resources and assets. It is the feeling of *going for it* that makes it so exciting. It makes the payoff so much more rewarding.

In entering this entrepreneurial world, Terry had to assess for himself, "Is it worth the financial and emotional risk?" As he thought about it, he knew he wanted to be his own boss, and he was used to living a life of uncertainty. He might call it chaos. He had the passion and energy to charge on. He determined, "As long as it's moral, ethical, and legal, I'm going for it."

Terry Duperon charged ahead into the entrepreneurial arena. He resigned from Trippensee. He was sacrificing predictability and a steady paycheck for the uncertainty of the entrepreneurial world.

Like many entrepreneurs, Terry's skills were based on his creativity in inventing products, and services filling a need of customers. He was brilliant in this domain. What Terry lacked was managerial adeptness (most entrepreneurs fit into this description). He didn't go to business school and read very little because of his dyslexia. He paid dearly for these deficiencies in spite of the fact that he designed and produced great products.

I digress into my sphere of philosophy to talk about creating a better world! This is the domain of inventors. Inventors are all about bringing something into this world that doesn't presently exist.

Terry's spiritual approach to opportunities was addressed by two of the world's most respected philosophers: Sir Issac Newton and Alfred North Whitehead. Their insights differed with regard to the concept of our partnership with God in creating a better world. Terry's approach aligns with that of Whitehead.

In the fifteenth century, English mathematician, physicist, astronomer, theologian, and author Sir Issac Newton posited that *God created a perfect world, perfect in every way — except for human beings.* According to Newton, given the chance, human beings will mess up God's otherwise-perfect world. His message was that people need to be closely supervised.

This thinking still exists in organizations that have layers of leadership hovering over people with close supervision to ensure that they don't mess up their otherwise-perfect businesses.

In the nineteenth century, English mathematician and philosopher Alfred North Whitehead stated that he disagreed with Newton's belief that humans, given the chance, naturally fall into destruction rather than creation. Whitehead advanced the theory that *creation is on-going, and humans are co-responsible agents with God in creating better people, better homes, better transportation, better businesses — a better world.*

From the perspective of being a co-responsible agent with God, Terry gained the confidence necessary to enter the entrepreneurial world and forge ahead on a fearless, but sometimes vulnerable, pathway. He was willing to take the necessary risks of criticism and possible failure. While he was willing to share the glory of success with the Holy Spirit who provides inspiration and insights into the next clear step, he always knew that he had to do the work.

On April 23, 1910, Theodore Roosevelt gave what would become one of the most widely quoted speeches of his career. The speech was called "Citizenship in a Republic" and has since come to be known as *The Man in the Arena*. Attacking the cynics who looked down at men who were trying to create a better place, he said, "The poorest way to face life is to face it with a sneer — a cynical habit of thought and speech, a readiness to criticize work which the critic himself never tries to perform, an intellectual aloofness which will not accept contact with life's realities — all these marks, not... of superiority but of weakness."

Then he delivered an inspirational and impassioned message that drew huge applause:

> It's not the critic who counts; not the man who points out how a strong man stumbles, or where doers of deeds could have done them better. The credit belongs to the man who is actually in the arena, whose face is marred by dust and sweat and blood; who strives valiantly; who errs,

who comes short again and again, because there is no effort without error and shortcoming; but who does actually strive to do the deeds; who knows great enthusiasms, the great devotions; who spends himself in a worthy cause; who at the best knows in the end the triumph of high achievement, and who at worst, if he fails, at least fails while daring greatly, so that his place shall never be with those cold and timid souls who neither know victory nor defeat.

Terry didn't let having some sort of learning disability stand in his way. Like a bullfighter, he functioned on instinct and intuition, with a measure of fear thrown in. He knows that he learns and thinks differently but he is used to working hard as a way of compensating for what he lacks.

One of Terry's outlooks is "Go with what you've got!" He has a very strong work ethic. As his dad told him early on, "You might not be able to read, but that doesn't stop you from working hard." Terry refuses to be an outsider, watching the action with his nose pressed to the window.

Terry entered the arena of the entrepreneurial world in 1976 when he started B&K Pump. He asked for and got the blessings of Jacob Becker and Val Kostrzewa, the owners of B&K Tool and Die, for permission to use their B&K name, as they were familiar with the pump Terry had invented and saw promise in both Terry and his product.

B&K Pump Corporation

TERRY L. DUPERON
TEL. (517) 753-5131
OR (517) 753-1437

945 S. TOWERLINE RD. • SAGINAW, MICHIGAN 48601

Becker and Kostrzewa each invested $5,000 for shares in Terry's business venture. With the B&K endorsement and that initial investment, Terry was able to sell shares that produced about $200,000 in working capital. Terry aggregated twenty-six stockholders.

B&K
6" Submersible Pump

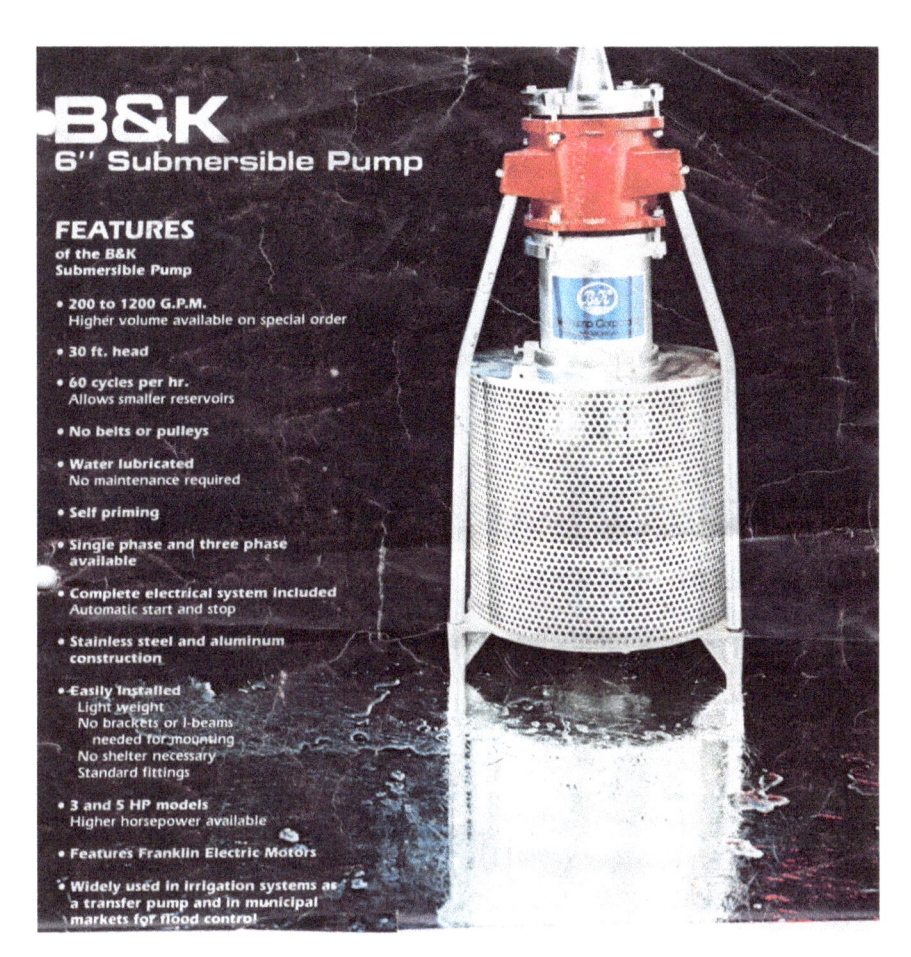

FEATURES
of the B&K
Submersible Pump

- 200 to 1200 G.P.M.
  Higher volume available on special order
- 30 ft. head
- 60 cycles per hr.
  Allows smaller reservoirs
- No belts or pulleys
- Water lubricated
  No maintenance required
- Self priming
- Single phase and three phase available
- Complete electrical system included
  Automatic start and stop
- Stainless steel and aluminum construction
- Easily Installed
  Light weight
  No brackets or I-beams needed for mounting
  No shelter necessary
  Standard fittings
- 3 and 5 HP models
  Higher horsepower available
- Features Franklin Electric Motors
- Widely used in irrigation systems as a transfer pump and in municipal markets for flood control

B&K brochure for a farm pump

B&K Pump sold pumps and related services initially to farmers who needed to install tubing into their fields to pump the water into ditches. Terry was then able, facilitated by the sales efforts of Bob Premo, who had left B&K to help with Terry's endeavor, to get some city and county contracts.

Fortunately, one of the relationships Bob

was able to secure was with Saginaw County Drain Commissioner James A. Koski (hereafter referred to as Koski). He and Terry became friends through Bob. Koski contracted with B&K Pump to install pumps, maintain pump stations, and do routine maintenance on pumping equipment.

Terry came to Koski with an idea that would possibly save Koski from spending his nights removing debris at pumping stations. Whenever there would be a big storm, the pumping equipment became useless as debris came up against the screen. So, typical of the way Terry processes a problem and true to his desire to limit complexity, he stood right in the channel, watched how debris came to the passive screen, and designed a simple mechanical tool to fix the problem: the first self-cleaning trash rack. Terry's request was to allow him to install an experimental prototype of the trash removal system. Part of Terry's offer was that if the trash rack worked, he would only charge Koski for his material design.

Terry's napkin sketch

The trash rack Terry designed and installed at the Saginaw-Zilwaukee Pumping Station has the capability of handling approximately ninety- to one-hundred-thousand gallons of stormwater per minute. That trash rack is still working fifty years after installation, with only two rather simple modifications. I suggested to Terry, "Maybe you should have paid more attention to building planned obsolescence into your products."

Koski was the first to purchase Terry's self-cleaning trash rack. Terry's patent was referred to by Koski as Serial Number 1, because they found that it is hard to sell the first prototype of anything. From that point on, Terry gave higher serial numbers to all of his inventions.

On another front, Terry was finally able to muster up the courage to divorce Jackie. At this point, his business was up and running, his spiritual life was thriving, he was more involved in the lives of his kids, and he had sworn off love and marriage... and then came Leslie.

11

LESLIE AND TERRY'S COURTSHIP

Terry navigated through his divorce for about two years before it was finalized. Terry committed to spending a great deal of time with his children because he was seeking full custody. He literally took them everywhere.

Because of his stress-filled marriage with Jackie, he was not ready for, nor was he interested in, getting married again. Casual and short-term relationships were all he had to offer. This attitude led to lots of one-time dinner-and-movie dates. Most often there was little or no chemistry between them, and some of his dates were simply friends who needed a companion to go to a wedding, a funeral, or some other gathering.

One morning, as Terry says, "I stood in front of the mirror, naked, and I wondered, 'What woman would want this man? I am out of shape, responsible for five children, and practically broke.'"

Terry's relationship with Jackie had been driven, from the very beginning, by hormones. Terry was hoping to find that same intensity of chemistry again. Well, that didn't happen, but something even better did. Terry met Leslie Cheryl Ross.

As a very young girl, Leslie showed a nurturing spirit. She saved a childhood picture of herself, sitting on a couch holding her three dolls, oddly named Susanna, Susan, and Suzy. She loved playing "mom" to her dolls. And, later, when two younger siblings were added to the Ross family, Leslie truly enjoyed caring for her younger sisters. Her dream of motherhood was already forming at that early age.

The first contact between Terry and Leslie happened in November of 1978 via a telephone call that was orchestrated by Terry's friend, Bob Premo. Terry sponsored a softball team that Bob Premo coached and Leslie's friend Annie played for. Annie was the bookkeeper and Leslie was the receptionist at Michigan Bean Shippers Association. They worked well together, ready and willing to combine work with fun.

According to Leslie, "Bob Premo was a nut. He would call Annie to let her know when and where the next softball game would be. On some of these calls, he would tease me before I passed the call on to Annie. For example, he would pretend to order a pound of beans. He knew that our business did not sell beans, but he liked to mess with me." Leslie knew how to cope with Bob because her father had been a horrible tease.

Annie's desk was located in a space near Leslie's, and the window in front of Annie's desk provided a view of the entryway. Annie would always warn Leslie when anyone was coming in. One day, Bob came in and before he even got through the door, he asked Leslie, "Are you married?" She answered, "No," then Bob asked, "Do you want to get married?" After a period of hesitation, Leslie said, "Sorta." Bob immediately picked up the phone, called Terry, and said, "I've got a girl here who is dying to meet you," and then he handed the phone to Leslie.

Terry thought he was speaking with Annie; after several minutes of embarrassed banter, he said, "Annie, you sound nervous." Leslie quickly replied, "I'm not Annie, this is Leslie. Do you want to talk to Annie?" Terry said, "Yes."

Terry then chatted with Annie for a few minutes, trying to get a description of Leslie. Leslie could hear Annie saying, "Blonde hair, about five-foot-four." Then Annie put Leslie back on the phone. Terry offered, "After all I have put you through, I'd like to take you out to lunch." This was on a Friday and they agreed to meet on Monday at noon at Treasure Island Bar and Restaurant in Saginaw.

Leslie was nervous about their upcoming date. She hardly knew what to expect. Leslie says, "I was painfully shy and introverted; I had had less than ten dates in my life, and I was twenty-six years old. I never had the courage to introduce myself to a stranger. The friends I did have had either sat next to me in school or were people I worked with on a daily basis."

Terry carried around this photo of Leslie, taken before they began dating, for a long time after they were married.

    Leslie had never been to Treasure Island, but she knew where it was. She drove her fourteen-year-old big Oldsmobile Dynamic Eighty-Eight to their meeting. The paint on the car was discolored and there was ample rust. Hoping to avoid embarrassment, when she arrived at Treasure Island, she parked her car out of sight by the railroad tracks.

Leslie says, "I was almost hyperventilating as I entered the restaurant. My thought was, 'How will I know him?' He said he would be wearing a three-piece navy blue suit, just like everybody else, so that was not much help. I walked up to the only man whose back was toward me. Fortunately, it was Terry.

"Terry was looking at something on the wall. I walked up to him and asked, 'Are you Terry?' Terry responded with, 'Yes. Are you Leslie?'" The two were ushered to a table and began to talk.

Leslie remembers, "As we had lunch, we immersed ourselves in conversation and I completely lost track of time. I left the office at 11:30 a.m. My lunch hour was from 12:00 p.m. to 1:00 p.m.

"I didn't get back to the office until 2:00 p.m. It was not at all like me to extend my lunch hour, and while it happened only that one time, my boss reminded me that my lunch was only one hour for the next five years.

"We had enjoyed our conversation and had lost track of time. Terry told stories, showed me pictures of his kids, and asked me questions about my life. One of his questions was 'What is your dream?'"

Leslie wished she had had a clever answer ready but she didn't. She had been thinking that her dream might never be realized. She had taken different jobs and even moved, hoping to find the right man, but there was always a reason to come back home.

Fortunately, however, earlier that very week she had invested several hours analyzing her life. This was the result of being so mad at God. "I had always done what I felt God wanted me to do. I had taken several jobs, even moved to New York State. At the age of twenty-six, I was still single and my last friend had just gotten married. I blamed God for still being single, so I sat down to analyze my past, my motives, my life.

"With legal pad in hand, I began to look at everything that had anything to do with me:

- Why haven't I met Mr. Right?
- How would I ever meet the man of my dreams?
- What do I really want out of my life?

"Deep within me was the question, 'Why am I mad at God?' I had nurtured my two little sisters and babysat lots of children. Therefore, when I found out there was a teacher shortage, I thought pursuing a degree in education and working with children would be a good career choice. I had a four-hundred-dollar-per-semester grant, but I quickly realized it would cost my parents a great deal beyond that amount over the four years it would take to complete my degree. I didn't want my parents to bear the burden of those costs. Furthermore, I began to question if I really wanted to stay in college to be a teacher, and spend the rest of my life in a classroom. I was in a quandary, and ended up dropping out of college for the time being, and went to work as a private secretary and a receptionist.

"I liked these jobs that ranged from

working at Mahon Industrial to working for attorneys, but I wasn't able to earn enough money to make a nice living for myself, so I enrolled in nursing school. However, nursing school did not suit me either and when I contracted mononucleosis, I had to leave the program. I never ended up going back.

"I applied for several jobs after I was better, and finally landed a job with Michigan Bean Shippers Association, located in the mostly-empty Eddy Building. Our office was on the fifth floor and it was dark, dingy, and in an unsafe part of the old downtown Saginaw area."

Once Leslie had finished her self-analysis, she realized, "All I really wanted was to get married and raise children in a happy, healthy household. This was a departure from the current desire of many young women who wanted to pursue a career. While I was enjoying some aspects of each of my jobs, my heart and my identity were not really in any of them."

Because all of this was so fresh in her mind, Leslie summarized her response to Terry's question about her goals by saying, "All I really want is to get married, have children, and live a good family life."

Leslie immediately regretted the answer she had given when Terry emphatically responded, "I'm not getting married for another ten years!" Leslie says, "I hated to hear that. Fortunately, we didn't linger in that conversation, we just kept talking about interesting things in our lives.

"After lunch, I felt like I was floating. I loved the way Terry talked about his family. I think he was reluctant to tell me he had five kids, but when their pictures fell out of his wallet, he shared his story. His sharing made me feel very comfortable. I was not fidgety, and I didn't feel like I was talking too much or too little. It felt like, *Wow — someone I can be myself with!*

"As we left the restaurant, Terry insisted on walking me to my car. He didn't say anything about the huge old faded rust bucket. He didn't even mention the fact that I had cattails in the back seat and that they had exploded, shedding furry-like stuff all over. Why did I have cattails in the back seat of my car? The answer is simple. I had so little money and only the basics when it came to furniture in my small apartment. I had gathered cattails from ditches with the plan of putting them in vases as decorations for the apartment. Then, I forgot about them. It was embarrassing to have Terry see this mess. He made no mention of it, and I appreciated that.

"I credit Terry's uplifting way of dealing with life with helping me to shed my extreme shyness. We agreed on a second date for the very next day."

Leslie saw Terry in a very different light than how Terry saw himself. She saw a real man, one who took his children to church and engaged with them; one who visited with his mom, making sure everything was ok in her life. She saw the core of who Terry was. She was not bothered by the fact that he had five kids. In fact, she was very impressed by the way he took care of them. She liked the fact that he was a church-going man. Socially, he would have a drink or two, but he clearly was not a big drinker. Perhaps, most importantly, he treated her like a lady and was sincerely impressed that, from a very early age, Leslie had envisioned herself as a wife and mom, living a good family life.

Some of the things Terry saw in Leslie began to occupy more and more of Terry's thoughts. In his words, "I couldn't stop thinking about her, and all these years later, that is still true. I have come to believe that you fall in love with someone long before you meet them. Little traits you have learned from your mother and others whom you admire show up in someone and you find yourself falling in love." As these traits showed up in Leslie, Terry fought it at first, but he was drawn to what Leslie brought to the relationship like a moth to a flame.

> *The first time that he saw her*
> *He knew everything had*
>   *changed*
> *Overnight love started blooming*
> *Like the first rose of spring*
> *Auburn hair like a sunrise*
> *Sweetest smile he'd ever seen*
> *Butterflies, they danced*
>   *around her*
> *Like the first rose of spring*

*Summertime would've never
    started*
And wintertime would never end
*She colored his life, opened
    his eyes*
To things he'd never dream
Without the first rose of spring
Gave him children like a garden
*They gave 'em all the love
    they'd need*
*To grow up strong, she made
    a home*
And every year he'd bring
Her the first rose of spring

— Willie Nelson

Leslie meant that much to Terry. As Leslie began to occupy more and more of his thoughts, he knew that his life would be forever changed.

Leslie remembers, "Here I was, living in a sparsely furnished apartment, surviving from paycheck to paycheck. My uncle Dave had sold me the old car I was driving for four hundred dollars and the furnishings in my apartment were a combination of things I had been given or items thrown away by other people that I had picked up by their curbs. Dad helped me fix some broken things and paint other things.

"I had to carefully choose how I spent my money, so I was very frugal. I shared these thoughts with Terry. He clearly knew I was struggling, but so was he.

"After we had dated for a few months, I felt we were headed in the direction of getting married. Then, to my surprise, after we had enjoyed dinner at Terry's family's home, Terry asked me, 'What would you say if I told you I still wanted to wait for ten years to get married?' I took a deep breath and then responded without hesitation, 'I'd have to be on my way then.'

"In the time between Terry asking me that question and Easter, Terry would put his arm around me as if to ask me a question, but then he would not say anything. By this time, I had started attending a new church and had joined the choir."

During this time Terry remembers feeling conflicted. Of course he had doubts about getting married again, after his marriage with Jackie had turned out to be much less than perfect. However, there was something he found different about Leslie. They enjoyed being together and he didn't feel like he had to hide anything from her. He wondered "Is this what it feels like to love and be loved back?"

One night while Leslie was preparing to go to choir practice, Terry called her and asked Leslie to call him right after she was done with practice. Terry had made several calls with the intention of telling her he had changed his mind about waiting ten years to get married. Yet, with each call he would lose his nerve. He had made up his mind that, this time, he would overcome his fear of committing to their relationship. However, the ominous phone call Leslie received from Terry did not convey his intentions.

Leslie says, "This phone call put me on edge for the duration of choir practice, especially since Terry had asked me if I could wait another ten years for marriage. As soon as I returned home, I called Terry. He responded by saying he couldn't talk right then. I found that very disturbing and I was afraid that he wanted to break up with me. I was so upset that I went to my room for the remainder of the night. Terry called me back a few hours later and it came out that he did not want to break up. He said, 'No no no, it's just the opposite.' I remember being so relieved."

The night before Easter, Terry managed to work up the courage to propose. Leslie says, "He put his arm around my shoulder and declared, 'I want you to be my wife.'

"My response was a tentative 'No,' and when Terry asked me why, I told him, 'I never want to be bored.' My life prior to meeting Terry had been pretty boring. I really wanted to marry Terry, but I wanted some assurance that life with him would not be boring. He then said, 'I can guarantee you will never be bored!'" It appears that both Terry and Leslie had the pre-dissonance that most couples have when making the decision to marry, i.e., "Am I sure I want to do this?"

Terry says, "We became engaged but there wasn't a lot of romance involved. I never got down on one knee and couldn't afford an engagement ring. And the first time I kissed

Leslie, it was like a dad kiss." Leslie laughs as she says, "Terry's daughter Laura and I went and picked out a ring together. There was no diamond." Later, Terry took a diamond that had been given to him by his uncle and put it in her ring.

During the year leading up to their marriage, Leslie (and to some degree Terry) met with a lot of outside resistance. Leslie received unwelcomed advice from several sources, all suggesting she was making a terrible mistake in marrying Terry, even though they had never met Terry.

Leslie received months of letters, literally one a week, from a longtime friend, listing all kinds of objections to Terry, particularly the fact that he had been divorced. The pastors of several churches had refused to marry Terry and Leslie because he had been married before. Terry's Catholic priest required six months of planning, but the preparations were already in the works and the date had been set. A church friend invited Leslie to lunch at her house, and Leslie was excited to attend because her friend had a newborn and she had not yet met him. To Leslie's total shock and dismay, this event was actually a planned intervention to talk her out of marrying Terry. As Leslie was leaving the get-together, she was told, "Save the stamps, don't even send us invitations."

At the same time, a coworker was planning a bridal shower for Leslie. Forty or fifty people were invited, but only one or two showed up. This was the straw that broke the camel's back with respect to Leslie's friends. It began to dawn on her what a true crossroads she was encountering. She really had to choose: her friends, or Terry.

As Leslie shared the story of the humiliation she suffered over the intervention, Terry's feelings toward her friends were spiraling downward at an advancing pace as well. His response initially was, "Are they really your friends?" However, as he thought more deeply about it, he said, "If we step back, perhaps they are simply doing what they have been taught to believe." Leslie says, "Terry's wisdom really helped me cope."

As Terry reflects on that time in his life, he now better understands the objections Leslie's friends had toward their marriage. In his words, "All of Leslie's friends were conservative, and my profile violated nearly all of their beliefs: I was divorced, Catholic, I had five children, and I was a smoker. I also occasionally drank alcohol. Truly, it seemed to them like I was at the bottom of the barrel."

Leslie's parents were not church-goers and they smoked. So, Leslie did not share all of the same beliefs to the same degree as her friends had been raised to believe.

Oddly enough, when Leslie went to Sunday school with her brother, she would then attend church by herself since her brother would go home right after Sunday school. Not one person welcomed her at the door or talked to her when she sat down for the service. In spite of these things, Leslie went anyway. She regularly attended that same church until she was twenty-five years old.

Leslie saw things in Terry that she really valued. As she says, "I saw Terry as an adult. His conversations focused on his children and his mom. Terry often visited his mother and always looked for ways to help her."

When Leslie was as young as sixteen, she

started praying that God would mold her and her husband so that they would fit each other. In her mind, Terry matched up well with respect to all of the most important qualities she hoped for in a husband. First and foremost, she saw Terry as a family man, and that was very important to her.

Leslie had always hosted a dream of spending her life as a mother and a wife. She was not career-oriented. Terry's response to this was that he had enough ambition for both of them, and she could see that.

After getting engaged, Terry soon realized what real love and commitment felt like. His love for Leslie was one that was very unlike what he had felt for Jackie. Terry felt a responsibility to marry Jackie because she was pregnant, but not because he was in love with her. This led him to seek and achieve an annulment for his marriage to Jackie. The church authorities agreed, as the only reason the two were married in the first place was due to their bringing a child into the world. On November 14, 1979, the annulment came through. Terry finally felt like his chapter with Jackie was over and he was ready to begin a new love story with Leslie and his five kids.

As Terry approached the wedding, the only real resistance he experienced was from his children, and it was unspoken resistance. As they say, "Actions speak louder than words," and Terry's kids were not willing to accept Leslie as their new mom. In essence, they treated her with some disregard. For example, she would make a crockpot dinner that was all ready to eat and some of the kids would make a sandwich. Also, since Terry had gained full custody, the children had become accustomed to spending a great deal of time with him and, for the most part, they enjoyed that. Now, Terry was spending more time with Leslie, and he would soon be bringing someone new into their household. They were not really happy about that. Leslie thought her relationship with the children would be like *The Sound of Music*. It didn't turn out that way.

Prior to the wedding, Terry recalls saying to Leslie, "'As long as I know you, I will not try to change a hair on your head. And I don't want you to try to change a hair on mine.' I also told her that I have a mother and I don't want to be mothered. I also have daughters and I don't need another daughter. What I do want is to have someone to walk through this life with me and take on whatever comes."

12

HERE COMES THE BRIDE

As Terry watched Leslie walking down the aisle with her father, he vowed, *I will never criticize this woman for as long as she lives. She has made it to age twenty-seven without my input, and I am sure she can make it through the rest of her life without it.*

Terry says, "I made this vow because, throughout my childhood, my parents bickered from dawn until dusk, and during my marriage to Jackie, we were always on each other's case. I wanted no more of that in my life. I felt that if you can't criticize, you can't manipulate, so there is no point in finding fault."

Leslie valued Terry's outlook because "my father was a terrible tease and my mother was a bit of a nag. My family's unease didn't even come close to that which took place during Terry and Jackie's marriage." Her mom and dad did not bicker as they did, but Leslie's temperament didn't react well to even minor arguments. "My sisters bickered incessantly. I would find a way to get away."

Terry says, "When I pushed away from finding fault, I began to see the core of the woman God had created in Leslie. Over time, I also began to see less fault in myself and in others, and began to look for what I call *the core of a person* — the person God created. The core is the deepest part of you. I find it by observing the things a person loves and cares about, what feeds them, what matters to them."

Terry had this model made to remind him of the symbolism of marriage: two whole, complete people, equal in stature, doing the work of life together.

Terry says, "Later in our marriage, I thought of our marriage from the perspective of a team of two horses pulling a wagon: man and wife team up, whole and complete and of equal stature. They hook up to the same wagon. They throw their hopes and dreams in the wagon and head out through life to take on whatever comes. One can pull the whole load, but only for a short time."

According to Terry, "For me, the first few months of marriage presented a serious period of adjustment. Simple things, but things I wasn't used to accommodating: I was not used to showing common courtesy when I was the king. I never had to tell anyone I would be late for supper or say what I was up to. I found that Leslie expected me to let her know."

From left: Jeff, Laura, Mike, Tammy, Terry Jr.

According to Leslie, "As soon as Terry showed me that he would sometimes be late for supper or other things, I simply thought to myself that he was not going to be like my dad. My father operated like clockwork, always home by 4:30 p.m. If Terry was late, I would just tell the kids that perhaps someone wanted to talk to him. I remember one kid saying, 'Why would anyone want to do that?'

"There were so many things I needed to get used to. Perhaps the biggest was adjusting to the attitudes and behaviors of Terry's children.

"When I think back about the kids, it must have been difficult for them, too. They were older and they weren't about to call me 'Mom.' I was providing what I felt the kids needed. I cooked for them and did other motherly things. Mostly, I tried to stay out of their way. I knew I was doing things that they needed, things they were not used to. I wanted to provide a place of safety at home, hot meals, and other things."

Terry's son, Jeff, seemed to sum things up from the children's perspective: "Leslie tried to help but she pretty much stayed in the background. It was a no-win situation for her. We weren't used to being mothered, and we weren't going to take it from her. She did the best with what she could."

"Terry and I tried to provide stability and predictability for our family," Leslie continued. "Terry did the laundry and I took care of the food. Using a slow cooker accommodated the differing schedules of the kids. This allowed them to eat at times convenient to them. I discovered that some of the kids were so used to fending for themselves that they would cook whatever they wanted on their own, even if dinner was ready for them.

"As I watched Terry's children grow and become accustomed to our new lifestyle, I felt the need to bear and raise children of my own. I was worried about confronting Terry about my dream. He already had five children. Of course we talked about having more children before I married him. But I wondered if he still wanted more?"

Producing children turned out to be a little more difficult than Terry or Leslie thought. It took five years before becoming pregnant with their first child together, Maggie, but when Leslie discovered she was expecting, "it was like a dream come true. All kinds of emotions — joy, anticipation, and also some terrifying thoughts that produced claustrophobic episodes." For example, she felt like the world was closing in on her and she couldn't breathe. She would go to the window and put her head out to get some air.

Witnessing Maggie's birth caused a quick bonding for Terry that he had not experienced with the birth of his other children. Up until about the 1980s, fathers were not invited in to watch the actual birth. With all of his children born before Maggie, his first sight of them was of a small fragile baby wrapped in swaddling clothes. He was deeply moved when he heard Maggie's first cry, and he was really surprised at how rough she was handled — held upside down by her feet and slapped on her bottom as the nurses did with most babies. Terry says, "I loved and still love all of my children, but with Maggie, it was love at first sight," because of his witnessing the miracle of birth up close and personal. When Maggie was placed on Leslie's stomach after her birth, Leslie said, "Let's call her Megan." Terry agreed, but to this day he still calls her Maggie.

Leslie shares, "It was a beautiful sight to see Terry sitting on the couch with his legs stretched out in front of him with Maggie resting on his legs and both sleeping soundly." Somewhat surprisingly to Terry and Leslie, the two children who were still living at home, Laura and Michael, seemed to really enjoy holding and playing with baby Maggie.

Abbey was born four-and-a-half years later. Leslie received two epidurals, but neither had any effect. The decision was made to put Leslie under and perform a Cesarean section. Terry got to hold little Abbey right away, while it was several hours before Leslie was able to take her into her arms. Terry bonded immediately with Abbey, but with Leslie, it took more time because she was unable to hold her.

Terry and Leslie were really committed to doing their best in raising their two girls to feel safe, loved, and capable. They would be spared the more difficult upbringing experienced by Terry's first five children.

I recorded the following cover song of "Look at Us" by Vince Gill on my recent album, *A Soft Place to Fall*. It brought tears to the eyes of Terry and Leslie because it so closely related to their life together:

> *Look at us*
> *After all these years together*
> *Look at us*
> *After all that we've been through*
> *Look at us*
> *Still leaning on each other*
> *If you wanna see how true love*
>   *should be*
> *Then just look at us*
> *Look at you*
> *Still pretty as a picture*
> *Look at me*
> *Still crazy over you*
> *Look at us*
> *Still believing in forever*
> *If you wanna see how true love*
>   *should be*
> *Then just look at us*
> *In a hundred years from now*
> *I know without a doubt*
> *They'll all look back and*
>   *wonder how*
> *We made it all work out*

Chances are we'll go down in
    history
When they wanna see
How true love should be
They'll just look at us

A recent photo of Leslie

Like all marriages, Terry and Leslie each face personal challenges, difficulties in raising their children, and financial issues from time to time, but they always live by the theme of two equally-capable horses pulling the wagon filled with their hopes and dreams. Therefore, if one of them went down, the other could pull the wagon alone for a while. This is the story of their marriage.

13

THE "EIGHTEEN AND OUT" RULE

A wise woman once said, "There are only two lasting bequests we can hope to give our children. One of these is roots, the other wings."

— Hodding Carter

Terry and Leslie's marriage was a living, breathing representation of what the song "Look at Us" manifests. They did, however, have challenges. The first serious challenge was how Leslie would choose to deal with the children from Terry's first marriage that were still at home.

Leslie chose to stay out of their way while doing things that she believed would accommodate them. "I thought of myself as kind of a college roommate, but emotionally I got attached to all of them. While I knew how to love them, it was too early for them to return my love in kind."

Terry's oldest five children receiving company jackets for Christmas

When Terry and Leslie married, Tammy

was seventeen; Terry Jr. was fifteen; Jeff was fourteen; Laura was thirteen; and Michael was nine years old. This family did not turn out to be the Brady Bunch. Even though Jackie had left, the quarreling and behavioral challenges among the children continued. Leslie stayed out of all frays.

During the first few years of his marriage to Jackie, Terry established a mandate that each of the Duperon offspring would be out on their own once they reached the age of eighteen. Terry and Leslie chose to continue with that strategy. Terry says, "I believe that eighteen is the age when young adults should begin the next leg of their life's journey. Eighteen is the age when young adults can get a job, go to college. If a person is allowed to stay home until age thirty, they will face the same challenges as an eighteen-year-old when they do leave the nest." Terry's "eighteen and out" rule worked out for some. For others it generated anger and resentment.

Terry looked at his "eighteen and out" policy as a kind of delivery date for them to begin the next chapter in their lives. Terry says, "My job, my duty, was to get the kids ready to fly. Of course, some would have difficulty leaving the nest, but in my mind, at eighteen they wouldn't be listening to me anyway. My job was to do my best to get them airborne by eighteen years of age."

From left: Mike, Abbey, Laura, Megan, Jeff, Terry Jr., Tammy

Tammy was the first. She was eighteen when she had baby Sarah, who was about three months old when they moved into a place of her own. She got an apartment in Saginaw and moved through a variety of jobs. She worked for an eye doctor, in retail, and finally landed a good job as office assistant at

Bernier Cast Metals. During these early years, her quest to find her own way seemed to work.

Jeff, like Tammy, felt he was ready to leave the nest at eighteen. He started college and was ready to make a life of his own.

Laura and Michael had a more difficult time trying to fend for themselves. Each of them holds some resentment toward their dad because of his rule. They feel they were kicked out of the house, and expected to survive on their own before they had the ability and willingness to succeed. Michael says, "I was angry about being forced to leave." Laura says, "I was not prepared for beginning life on my own. I was not equipped to do so. I made lots of mistakes."

Terry Jr. says, "I didn't understand the rule. In his world, I knew Dad believed it was the best thing for us and would serve our best interests. I still don't agree, but now that I'm older, I can see my dad's perspective more clearly. It wasn't just to get us out of the house."

Maggie shared a few examples from her childhood that she feels helped prepare her for leaving the nest at the age of eighteen. By the age of sixteen, she had a job, her own checkbook, and was able to buy her own car. She had also learned such things as how to change a tire and make her own appointments. Maggie adds, "I learned a lot about how to be street smart from my dad, especially when he would take me on work trips. On the good side, I learned how to navigate through the airport, check into hotels, and make sure no one is around when getting off an elevator so I could safely enter my hotel room. Dad told me to always walk with confidence. He would also leave me by myself at the hotels while I was with him on work trips. I was able to swim the whole day. I had no cellphone or any way to reach him but he would occasionally send someone to check on me. These unannounced visits kind of aggravated me. Dad felt I was safe so I did too. I didn't feel like I needed to be checked on or protected."

Maggie felt prepared to leave home at eighteen. After leaving home, she bought her own house in Reese, Michigan, where she and her daughter Kennedy lived.

When asked if Maggie would use this "eighteen and out" rule on her children, she shared that she would do something similar, but would like her children to just have a plan for what they would want to do next (post-graduation).

When talking to Abbey, the youngest of the children, she had this to say: "I think that I was totally prepared. I knew 'eighteen and out' was going to happen and I think they had been preparing me from a young age for it.

"I remember my mom in the kitchen mixing meatballs, learning how to make meatloaf, or baking cookies. She had such patience with letting me help in the kitchen, always teaching and allowing me to help. Then at a fairly young age, six to eight, we got to make dinner for the family. I probably made ramen noodles or grilled cheese or something, but I was in charge. It was great! I had paying chores around the house that I could do: take out the trash at the house and down the driveway at Dad's office, mow the lawn, get mail, start and finish laundry. Yes, these are simple things, but they taught me responsibility. And if you know me, I don't pass up a good opportunity to make some money. Dead animal? Sure, I'll bury it... for a price! One time I even crawled under my dad's office to find a smelly dead animal. Guess what, there wasn't one... but I still made sure I got paid for my efforts!

"Around the time when I turned fourteen, it was time to take 'the trip with Dad.' What was the meaning of this trip? It meant I had to do the navigating. I had to find our way to the airport, get us to our terminal, figure out how to get to our hotel. At the time, I didn't really think much about it, but looking back, it was his way of teaching me how to travel and preparing me for when I did have to do this on my own.

"When it was time for me to move out, I knew I didn't want an apartment. I didn't want to waste my money; I wanted to buy a house. After a quick search, I was able to snag a quaint little house in Frankenmuth. Shortly after, I got a fun job waitressing at the Bavarian Inn Restaurant. Life was good!"

When questioned about whether she would apply the "eighteen and out" rule to her children, Abbey said, "Probably not. Will we let them stay home until they're in their mid-twenties? Probably not. Our kids are still young, two and six, so we have quite some time to figure out exactly what our plan will be.

"I believe Dad took time to make sure we had a place to move into. He took time to prepare us for this next step. He wanted the best for us, not to push us out to only fail. He wants all his children to succeed. With every marriage, you know how you were raised and you learn how your partner was raised. We talk about what we liked and what we didn't really agree with, and from that we will choose to maybe take bits and pieces from each and create something new that works for us."

Terry adds, "I believe Leslie and I did a much better job of preparing the younger kids, Maggie and Abbey, for beginning the next chapter of their lives. This happened because by then we had more resources. I was able to take them with me to trade shows that showed them what I did for a living. I helped them learn how to travel by themselves and other things I couldn't afford to do with my older kids. With each of my kids, I had the desire to successfully launch them from our family into the world of their choice. I did this *for* them — not to them."

The entire Duperon family, as adults: Megan, Terry Jr., Laura, Mike, Leslie, Terry, Jeff, Abbey, Tammy

What does the research say about when a young adult should move out of the family dwelling? First, these days it's no longer as common to move out at eighteen as it used to be. While legally kids are not entitled to live with parents after age eighteen, a May 2016 *Pew Survey* indicated that a record number of 32 percent of young adults live with their parents. A *Time* magazine article suggests that doing this provides financial breathing room for eighteen- to thirty-four-year-olds who are remaining home. For the first time in seventy-five years, living in Motel Mom is the most common living arrangement for eighteen-year-olds.

Leaving home is a challenging period in nearly everyone's life, fraught with conflicting feelings and needs: the earnest desire for independence and autonomy, alongside the fear of failure and continuing sense of dependency on parents. These challenges are most apparent when a young adult graduates from high school and reaches the age of eighteen.

Terry says, "I never doubted for a minute that my kids were ready and able to fly." Two key messages that Terry tried to convey to his children above all others were that he was always there, and that he believed, and wanted them to believe, "You can do this."

14

CAPTURING GOVERNMENT CONTRACTS

Terry successfully ran B&K Pump until 1984 when the company began to run into financial difficulties. The investors all walked away from the business, leaving Terry with all of the bills. While it looks like the stockholders failed Terry, it has to be recognized that the business was not profitable and that the twenty-six investors could not see any way that more investment would change that.

B&K Pump closed in 1985. Terry owed the Internal Revenue Service $25,000. He had a $20,000 bank loan. Therefore, all of B&K Pump's assets went to the bank.

Terry negotiated with the bank to let him keep the pump parts in exchange for his promise to continue to sell pumps off inventory.

On a Sunday, Terry went to the doublewide trailer, located on B&K property. He loaded it on his flatbed truck and took it home. Once discovered, the B&K people were upset, but Terry owned the building because of the deal he made with the bank.

Terry's relationship with Jim Koski strengthened as Koski used Terry to do preventive maintenance on the pump stations, thereby getting Terry some much-needed work. Terry was particularly impressed with Koski's political connections through Don Hare, Congressman Bob Traxler's chief administrative assistant, and all the way up to Jim Blanchard, who would become the governor of Michigan, with Koski serving as Blanchard's campaign manager in Saginaw County.

After B&K Pump closed, Terry had to start over. This would be a real test of Terry's bounce-back-ability. Terry's tenacity, energy, and ability to see how he could develop products that solved problems would serve him well. He simply had a unique way of thinking through design solutions based on his belief that the fewer mechanical parts there are, the better.

Terry's pathway back started with creating a new company. At this point, having suffered through the separation of partners in B&K Pump, he wanted no partners in this venture as he got started.

Leslie had given up her job when Maggie was born. When her retirement contributions were returned to her months later, Leslie offered the money to Terry to start Duperon Corporation.

Terry managed to sell two more self-cleaning trash racks to Commissioner Koski for pumping stations in the nearby towns of Zilwaukee and Carrollton. He also sold one trash rack to the Federal Bureau of Reclamation for the Oso Diversion Dam near Chromo, Colorado. The only notable modification from the original prototype was a changing of the angle of the trash rack to better retrieve the incoming debris.

Terry and Megan in the early days of Duperon Corporation in an upstairs bedroom "office."

But he needed bigger, more lucrative contracts.

To fill this need, he asked Jim Koski if he would be interested in being a sales representative. Koski knew this could be considered a conflict of interest, being that he was an elected official. Koski had to give considerable thought to what possibilities lay in front of him. Was there any way he could work with Terry?

At this time, Koski was a bit disillusioned with the county board over his management of the county's flood fighting efforts during the 1986 flood event that hit Michigan (Saginaw projected as the likely most devastated area in Michigan).

Saginaw County's Emergency Management Department appointed Koski as the manager of the flood fighting effort because of his knowledge of the storm water systems. This was a huge responsibility. In reaction to the projected flood waters, Koski orchestrated a massive response. He began by asking for Governor Blanchard's assistance. Blanchard flew into Saginaw on September 12, 1986, on a State Police helicopter, accompanied by the general from the National Guard and others. They did an aerial evaluation of the situation to combat what was about to happen.

Koski hired Spicer Engineering to survey the five-mile area that was most vulnerable to flooding (the low-lying areas of Saginaw and Zilwaukee cities on the west side of the Saginaw River, as well as Carrollton Township). He got the Corps of Engineers to truck in pallets of sandbags to be strategically placed along the projected dike location. He arranged with Bourdow Trucking to spot piles of sand to be used to fill sandbags. Then, Koski got on the radio and local television stations to ask for volunteers to bring shovels and meet in the Carrollton school parking lot, from where they would be transferred via Carrollton school buses to the work sites. Thousands volunteered to help. Local pizza parlors fed the workers for free, and donations of water and soda came from a variety of different sources.

The Bay City-based National Guard brought in personnel and equipment to help with the dike-building. As the National Guard departed, they took off with their car horns honking. People lined up on the streets. Some of them were crying. One bystander said, "It was like World War troops going through."

Terry's challenge was to keep the pump stations running — no easy task. Why? As an example, one problem at one pump station developed when Consumers Power, a source of natural gas and electricity for Michigan, turned the power off. The motors were underwater. Once the power was turned off, the water rose and flooded the motors halfway up. To deal with this challenge, Terry had to build a dam around one motor to enable him to pull the motor out and dry it. After reinstalling the motor, the pump would keep the water down off the other pumps. Once the motors were dry, Terry called Consumers Power and the electricity was restored. The motors were up and running again.

The flooding started on September 11, 1986, and reached a peak that was below the projected elevations. However, there would have been significantly more flooding had the dikes or the pumping equipment failed. The pumps and stormwater equipment in place operated through the storm event with only minor modifications. Terry and Koski both worked day and night through the storm. The area experienced non-stop rainfall over a thirty-day period. Although the storm didn't materialize as badly as projected, there was severe flood damage.

Afterwards, a lot of second-guessing happened by Monday-morning quarterbacks about how Koski managed it and the costs associated. Koski's critics worried that the flooding level came short of reaching the sandbags in some areas. They didn't want to pay the costs associated with that effort. This frustrated Koski, Terry, and those involved because their preventive measures had saved many homes and businesses from millions of dollars in damage.

While FEMA and the State of Michigan picked up 85 percent of the costs incurred, some county board members wanted to renege on a $35,000 debt to the contractors that had dropped everything in an effort to avert a disaster. This caused a rift between Koski and some of his board members. When the board told their attorney, Leo Borrello, to get a legal opinion on whether to pay the contractors, Borrello told them, "Pay the bill!"

The board reluctantly paid the bill but their resistance left a bad taste in Koski's mouth. This set the stage for Koski to seriously entertain the idea of entering the private sector or perhaps running for a state office.

It was during this second-guessing time frame when Koski began seriously weighing his options. He was approached by Terry about joining Duperon Corporation in some fashion. After a few meetings, they came to an agreement. What helped sway Koski in Terry's direction was the comfort he had experienced in working with Terry, and his conviction that he could easily show that Terry's trash racks would meet the needs of potential clients.

Terry wanted Koski to join Duperon for many reasons. First and foremost, he enjoyed working with him. They enjoyed each other's humor. Secondly, Terry knew that he had a full understanding of how the pumps and trash racks functioned; and finally, Terry valued Koski's political connections and work ethic.

Terry agreed to match Koski's current financial package. Koski would serve as the president of the newly-created trash rack division of Duperon Corporation. In response to a *Saginaw News* reporter's question as to why he made the decision to leave big government and enter the private sector, Koski said, "I didn't want to go through life saying, 'If I would have or could have… my life would be different today.'" He didn't want to live with regret of not trying the unknown adventure.

Koski first got to know Congressman Traxler as a result of a conversation he had with Traxler's administrative assistant. The assistant had mentioned to Koski that Traxler needed a convertible in which to ride for the many upcoming parades that political personalities were requested to attend.

Hola! Koski had a 1967 yellow Camaro convertible and he ended up being Traxler's driver in parades. This led to a very close friendship between Traxler and Koski. At that time, Congressman Traxler asked him, "Why in the world would you leave a promising political career to join the very small Duperon Corporation?" Koski responded by beginning to explain the value he saw in the self-cleaning trash rack Terry had invented. That discussion led to other conversations about the possibility of the trash racks solving some governmental debris removal challenges.

Traxler's staff enjoyed Koski's visits to their office because he violated all of the political protocols usually afforded to congressional leaders, and this entertained Traxler's troops. Terry adds, "When I accompanied Koski to visit Traxler's office in Washington, I found that Traxler's office staff really looked forward to Jim's visits because he was so good at entertaining."

For example, the first young staffer that Terry met said, "Who is Jim Koski? Everybody is saying Jim's coming." His funny comments lit people up with laughter. Another time when Koski and Terry were having a discussion with Traxler in a restaurant, a guy wearing big dark glasses and a trench coat that reached the floor walked by. Koski drew spontaneous laughter when he made the comment, "Must have been the last guy leaving the coatroom!"

Koski joined Duperon Corporation in April of 1987.

The early headquarters of Duperon Corporation: a double-wide trailer.

The *Saginaw Township Times* reported:

Terry L. Duperon, president and owner of the Buena Vista-based firm Duperon Corporation, said he is glad to have a commitment from Koski, who had been offered jobs with the company in the past but declined. "I really couldn't find a more qualified person," said Duperon. "I will expand my manufacturing business and give Koski control of what I will call the trash rack division." Terry adds, "I think I have the best possibility of success with him. I am quite excited about it. Koski's experience in government, disaster situations, the political system, and manufacturing makes him the ideal person to take over the trash rack division."

Koski walked away from the remaining year and a half of his third four-year term as Saginaw County's drain commissioner. He left the first-floor corner office of the Saginaw County Courthouse on a Friday, and started the next Monday morning at Duperon Corporation. His office consisted of an eight-by-ten space, with no window, in a double-wide trailer (Duperon Corporation's headquarters) on Terry's property in Indiantown. He had a telephone and a rolodex with no contacts in it. As he sat behind the desk — one that he had to bring from home — he thought, *What the hell have I done?*

15

A TURN FOR THE BETTER

After settling into his new digs, Jim Koski started attempting to sell the Duperon custom-built self-cleaning trash racks through his own statewide contacts, especially with fellow drain commissioners. Koski discovered that this product was an expensive solution, and only those facing an urgent and important problem would spend the necessary money for it. The purchase had to be put through a budget cycle, so it was never an immediate payment.

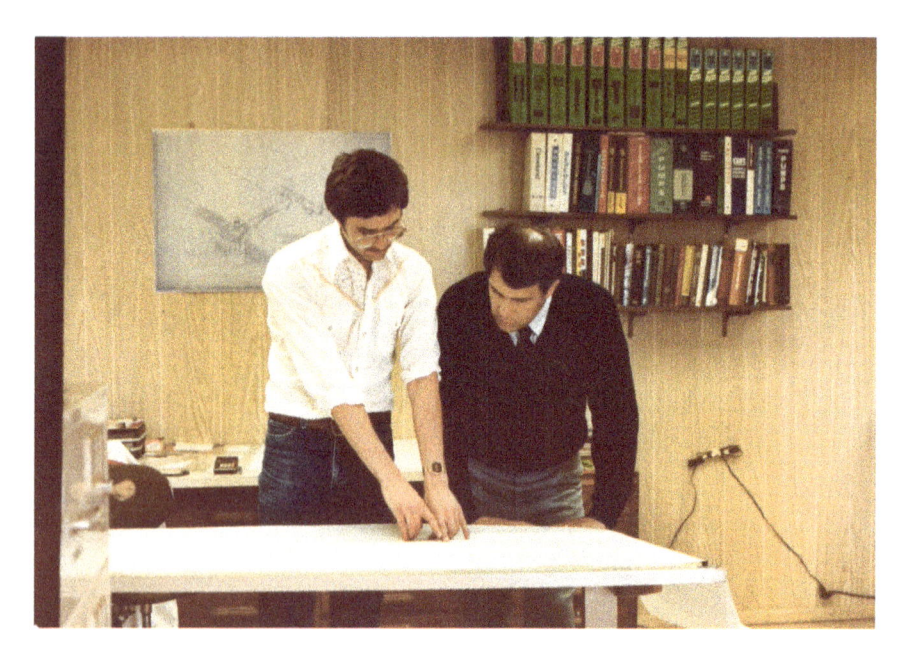

Jim Koski at work

This challenge made him think about the possibility of engaging the Corps of Engineers. He had worked with the Detroit District of the Corps on several occasions during his tenure as drain commissioner.

Koski knew the Corps of Engineers had built many stormwater pumping stations throughout the country. So he continued to discuss the possibility with Congressman Traxler about how to introduce Duperon's trash rack product to the Corps of Engineers on a trial basis. The idea of designing a demonstration project was born. This would enable pursuing a governmental project without competition.

Does this sound like cronyism? Yes? No? Maybe?

Koski did exploit his positive relationship with Senator Traxler to get things started. But, like it or not, this is how the wheels of government turn. People who are elected, in nearly all cases, have as their primary goal staying elected. To do this, they are constantly looking for ways to help solidify their value by bringing services and money to their districts. They encourage supporters to bring forth worthy ideas. Koski saw Terry Duperon's self-cleaning trash rack as a possibility worth exploring.

How any possibility gets through the system is frequently explained as follows: If you watched how sausages or policies are made, you wouldn't want either one. Admired for his humor, President Ronald Reagan offered, "It has been said that politics is the second oldest profession [the first being prostitution]. I have learned that it bears a striking resemblance to the first."

Traxler talked to his friend Hunter

Spillum, who had met Koski several times when Koski had visited Washington in past years. Spillum was a big gun within the United States Army Corps of Engineers. He was the civilian liaison to congress in charge of funding and projects for the Corps, and chief clerk for the congressional office of the Corps. His office was right around the corner from Traxler's office in the Rayburn Building.

Spillum had approached Traxler, seeking an opportunity for the Corps to do some engineering on NASA facilities. Traxler saw an opportunity to help Spillum in exchange for Spillum helping Koski get the introduction to the Corps that he needed. Traxler and Spillum discussed the possibility of assisting each other. They thought it best if Traxler were to meet with Terry and Koski to discuss their vision of what was possible.

As Terry tells it, Koski said, "Let's go to Washington, D.C., so you can meet with Traxler and see if he can assist us with our introduction to the Corps." This trip was not an unusual thing for Koski, because he did a yearly expedition that coincided with Congressman Traxler's April special election anniversary party. Koski would load up a van donated by Martin Chevrolet with locally-manufactured spirits from Geyer Brothers Brewery and a Frankenmuth wine store to provide Traxler's party with the necessary spirits to serve those attending.

Terry and Koski flew to Washington, D.C., and met with Traxler. Terry says, "Traxler was having a fundraiser the evening we arrived, and we were invited to attend as his guests." Although the price to attend this function was several hundred dollars per head, Koski and Terry were welcomed as non-paying guests. It amazed Terry that while all of the attendees had paid big sums to attend, not only did they get a free pass, Traxler spent lots of time with Koski and him.

After the fundraiser, Traxler (and his staff), Koski, and Terry went to the Dubliner Irish Pub, a favorite watering hole for politicos on The Hill. Over dinner, Terry and Traxler had a chance to get better acquainted. Traxler became more comfortable in moving ahead with what he had chatted about briefly with Hunter Spillum.

In follow-up discussions with Spillum and

at Traxler's recommendation, it was agreed that they needed a location where Duperon Corporation would be amenable to installing their trash rack to demonstrate to the Corps how well it would function. Koski began to look across the nation for facilities being designed by the Corps of Engineers that might benefit by the installation of Terry's self-cleaning technology.

About this time, Koski traveled to Louisville, Kentucky, to see his brother. While there, Koski secured an appointment with an engineer with the Louisville District of the Corp of Engineers. He explained how the trash racks worked and asked if the Louisville Corp had any need for such a system. Koski learned that the Corp was nearly finished with a project in Indiana and was told that, in order to install a trash rack, all they required was more funding. He agreed to try out the Duperon trash rack if Koski could come up with the needed funding. Koski was fired up.

When Koski returned to Saginaw, he told Terry about his potential deal. He had secured the project name and necessary numbers to forward to Traxler to see if it was possible to secure approximately $150,000 for the potential Louisville District project.

Traxler and Hunter Spillum were able to write the funding for the trash rack demonstration project into that year's Corps of Engineers appropriations bill. Once it's in the bill, it is published in the Congressional Record. When the Louisville District office discovered that a trash rack had been added to their pump station improvement project, the colonel and the chief engineer wanted to know, "How the hell did this happen?" The Louisville representative Koski had met with was over his skis, so to speak, when he told Koski they would use the Duperon screen if Koski found the money to pay for it. His bosses did not agree.

They summoned the Louisville project engineer to explain what happened. He told them, "This guy (Koski) came in and told me about his trash rack project and I said we could try it but we don't have the money for it. Then he asked me, what if he could get the money — would we try it? I guess I agreed."

The Louisville representative who had agreed that if Koski came up with the money they would proceed with the contract apparently did not have the authority to make such a commitment. He was overruled by his bosses. His bosses told him to get in contact with Koski to inform him that, even though he had gotten the money, they were not going to use it on that site. No deal for Duperon Corporation. Koski was devastated at the betrayal.

Yet the funding was now in the Congressional Record in the amount of $150,000, like an atheist dressed in his black suit in the coffin — all dressed up with nowhere to go. Similarly, Koski and Terry now had the money, but no project.

However, the bad fortune was about to take a turn for the better.

On hearing the news from Koski that the Indiana project was now moving forward without the trash rack, Traxler contacted Hunter Spillum and explained what had happened. They were close friends and had worked on many projects together. Since

Traxler was on the Appropriations Committee, Spillum frequently came to him for help on getting funding for things that would benefit the Corps. He was not pleased after all his efforts to get the funding approved. Spillum declared, "I will find out what can be done."

Annually, the Corps has a regional meeting of all its District offices to review all existing projects as well as the areas proposed for future development. At the next regional meeting of the Corps of Engineers that the Nashville and Louisville Districts were a part of, Spillum was seen having a spirited conversation with the general of the whole region. The essence of their conversation was that the Corps failed to follow the authorization in the Congressional Record to install the trash rack in Indiana. Spillum forcefully pointed out that the sponsor of the project was someone that, on many occasions, the Corps counted on for funding needed for Corps projects. This sponsor was Traxler. Spillum said, "Now we find out you're not going to use the trash rack. How am I expected to explain this to Congressman Traxler?"

Spillum and the general's rather heated conversation was overheard by the Nashville District colonel and his chief engineer, and they asked what was going on. When the situation was explained, their first question was, "What is a trash rack?" The answer received was, "Who cares? We gave the congressman our word and now we broke it." They told Spillum, "Leave the general alone. We'll put one in." They didn't have any idea what a trash rack was or what it did, but they bailed the general out.

The chief engineer of the Nashville District said, "We have a lot of water intakes in our district and we should be able to fulfill the commitment that was made to the congressman." After the Nashville reps committed to Spillum, they contacted Koski to learn about the trash rack and its capabilities. They invited Koski to come to their office to investigate potential sites for use of Duperon's Self-Cleaning Trash Rack system.

During this time, Koski had been diagnosed with throat cancer and was undergoing a tough regimen of radiation treatment. He worked as much as he could, but he had dropped one hundred pounds and was quite weak. He mustered up enough strength to board a plane and flew to Nashville. To his surprise, upon arriving at the Nashville airport, he was met by the colonel, the chief engineer, and a project engineer, all of whom reported to the general of the southern division. Unlike his first encounter with a Louisville District project engineer who worked on pump stations and had to report to higher-ups for all important decisions, Koski now had all the top-echelon decision-makers for the Nashville District working on finding a suitable location for the installation of an experimental trash rack.

They traveled together to look at all the potential sites. In their exploration of possibilities, the question was asked, "Would this system work on a dam?" Koski's answer was, "I don't know, but I will ask Terry."

They then visited the Cheatham Dam in Ashland City, just west of Nashville, on the Cumberland River. This was a three-turbine dam that generated electricity for the Nashville area. At first they said they would like to try it on one of the turbine intakes (75 feet wide and 65 feet high). It was certainly larger than anything Koski had contemplated. The Cheatham Dam was built in the 1930s, as part of many public service projects that were done to get the United States out of its depression. It was a low-head intake facility that had a lock system incorporated to allow for marine transportation. The higher the water level (referred to as head), the faster it turns the turbines, thereby generating more electricity. Conversely, if the head decreases, the slower the turbines turn, and less electricity is generated.

Jim Koski at the Cheatham Dam

The dam had a history of accumulating large amounts of debris — trees, barrels, dead animals, etc. — that would alter the efficiency of the production of electricity. The debris pileup was so thick that deer and people could actually walk on it. This was reducing the profitability of the hydropower production.

Koski and the Corps project engineer took measurements and gathered other information to allow the Corps to prepare a request for proposal (RFP) for a project. With pictures and dimensions of the Cheatham Dam in hand, Koski returned to Michigan a day later to meet with Terry to see if this project was even possible, knowing that the project would take a whole lot more than the agreed-upon $150,000 in the bill.

The initial plan was to try the trash rack on one of the three intakes to see how it worked. After a couple of days of calculating, and Terry pondering what it would take to do this, Koski got a call from Spillum, who said, "Do the whole thing!" This would bring the size of the trash rack to 225 feet wide by 65 feet high.

Duperon Corporation operated out of a double-wide trailer. They had no manufacturing facility. Could they meet the demands called for on this massive Cheatham Dam project?

16

AN UNBELIEVABLE WINDOW OF OPPORTUNITY

The request for Duperon Corporation to check the feasibility of installing a self-cleaning trash rack for twelve sections of the Cheatham Dam turbine intakes awakened Terry and Koski to the fact that they were entering into a domain beyond their wildest dreams.

Would the dream be a breakthrough to great things? Or would it end up being a nightmare? The question Koski posed to Terry, looking him straight in the eye, was, "Do you really think we can do this?" Terry looked back at Koski and simply smiled.

Terry's first look at the dam. At the time, he was so broke that he was wearing painter's pants (because they were inexpensive to purchase) with twenty-five cents in his pocket to cover his expenses on the drive home.

Not only did Terry have to come up with a design, he and Koski had to come up with specifications to meet the design requirements that would enable the Corps to put out an RFP that would enable a competitive bid.

According to Koski, "We needed to feature the uniqueness of our offer to gain an advantage over those who would compete for the bid on the Cheatham Dam project. We decided that our unique selling proposition was that our trash rack system would operate automatically and that it possessed the unique ability to remove a log up to sixty feet long and with a thirty-six-inch diameter, automatically." According to Terry, "We were confident that no competitor's trash rack system could do this. Our assessment proved to be correct."

After several months of visiting the dam, continuing discussions with operators of the dam, and visits to Saginaw by the Corps, a proposal was submitted for bids. The price tag: *five million dollars!*

According to Koski, "We then hit another 'eye-opening' moment. One specification for submitting a bid on this project was that everyone had to submit a performance bond [insurance that the contractor could fulfill his obligation] with their proposal. Then, if we did fail, the bonding company would insure the $5,000,000-plus would be provided to pay some other party to complete the project."

The Duperon Corporation had never needed to bond any projects and they did not have a relationship with a bonding company. This was a big challenge and it threatened their whole project.

DUPERON CORPORATION

SELF-CLEANING TRASHRACK

Cheatham Power Plant
Nashville, TN
1990

Debris: Logs, tires, container drums, animals

- 9 units: 25' W x 65' L

5693 Becker Road   Saginaw, MI 48601

The debris the dam collected was so large and the quantity of it was so immense that nothing on the market at the time could handle it.

It didn't take many phone calls to bonding companies to discover that there was not any way Duperon could get a bond to cover the expense of a project of this size. A bonding company is an insurance company. They have to pay if you don't successfully complete the project. They look at your liquidity (available money). Duperon Corporation had none. Neither did they have any history of completing any large projects.

Terry built a frame at Duperon Corporation to duplicate the dam site and test his invention. Being afraid of heights, it was a challenge to climb its sixty-five-foot ladder, but the testing paid off — the model worked!

It was a crisis that called for creativity. Koski made some calls. The only way he could see moving forward at the time was to partner with a general contractor with the bonding power to insure multimillion-dollar projects. The problem with that approach was that it would give control of all aspects of the project to whatever general contractor Duperon hooked up with. To both Terry and Koski, this was not a viable option.

Terry and Koski felt obligated to inform Congressman Traxler's office in Washington, D.C., of the inability of Duperon Corporation to acquire a bond. This meant they would need to become a subcontractor to the general contractor. According to Koski, "This was not a happy time. We had come so far and it seemed that this great opportunity was slipping away."

A couple of days later, Koski received a phone call from the project engineer that had been working within the Nashville office. To Koski's surprise and delight, this is what the engineer had to say: "Koski, I don't know who you know in Washington, but I do know that it must be someone very important. Our chief engineer just received a call from our commanding general telling him that this demonstration project is not going to require a performance bond." Then he added, "I've been with the Corps for over twenty years and I've never heard of not requiring a bond for such a large project."

Koski says, "After a couple of days, Duperon Corporation received an addendum waving the requirement for a performance bond. Duperon Corporation was back in action with smiles on their faces."

Terry worked out the numbers, and the final bid came to a little over $5.14 million. Terry later told Koski he figured out all the costs, then arbitrarily added another million dollars to cover what he possibly missed.

After the Cheatham Dam project received three bids, it was found that only the Duperon bid followed the exact bid specifications.

Once the bid was awarded, Terry and Koski had to focus on how to get the nine required trash racks built, delivered, and installed. Duperon Corporation had a young man who had just begun working as a utility guy, capable of doing many things. His name was Delmar Nichols. He agreed to take on the job as project superintendent. After visiting the site, he found there was no room there to fabricate the components. Therefore, he had to find a staging area as close to the site as possible to assemble the components. He located the needed site twelve miles upriver from the dam. In addition, he had to arrange for such things as transporting components out of Saginaw, and finding barges and tugboats to push the components down the Cumberland River to the job site. Then he had to secure a 300-ton ring crane to lift and place each of the nine 25-foot-wide, 65-foot-tall trash rack units in 45 feet of water.

Seven hard-hat divers were signed on to fasten the trash racks to the bedrock. These divers came from as far away as Australia. They had to be fully equipped and needed to have on-site access to a three-man decompression chamber. These men would be underwater for several hours per day. This required at least two hours in the decompression chamber after they surfaced to keep them from getting the bends. In the final analysis, these divers invested over 2,000 hours in the water without an incident.

Terry working on fixing the conveyer at the dam

Because of all the responsibilities Delmar assumed, Duperon Corporation rented a home near the site for the year and a half it took to complete the project. This home housed Delmar, his wife, and the crew from Saginaw.

Tammy working by hand to remove debris from the dam

Terry and Koski visited the site several times to help Delmar, and both were seriously impressed with the quality of Delmar's work. The project would never have been completed without Delmar.

Terry helping to install the trash racks

The Cheatham Dam project contract was awarded to Duperon Corporation by the Army Corps of Engineers on November 26, 1990. The $5.14 million project was completed on time and within budget on March 4, 1992. The final evaluation of the project was sent to Duperon Corporation on April 3, 1992. Here is a direct quote from the Corps of Engineer's final evaluation of the project:

> *Remarks of Outstanding Performance —*
> *The quality of work by Duperon was exceptional and they made quality improvements in their system without direction from*

the government. Management of the work was exceptional in that the work was performed and completed on time, which included over 2,000 hours of underwater work. Most decisions were performed with local management personnel which expedited the work.

Safety standards on the job were maintained at high levels and enforced by Duperon. Work included erection of steel members at elevated levels, complicated rigging procedures for setting the assembled trash racks, and over 2,000 hours of diving operation with no lost time accidents. Labor standards were adhered to and reviewed by Duperon regularly to assure compliance.

Koski, Terry, Delmar, and others were elated with the high praise for a job well done. One could easily conclude that Hunter Spillum and Congressman Traxler were equally pleased with the result. They had risked their reputations on this project.

With the trash racks installed, the Cheatham Dam project was complete.

With this complex multimillion-dollar project successfully completed, the new game for Duperon Corporation would be to go *elephant hunting* — finding new multimillion-dollar projects.

17

WHAT GOES UP MUST COME DOWN

The success of the Cheatham Dam project was sure to catapult Duperon Corporation into a whole new stratosphere — at any rate, it is what they hoped would happen. They might blissfully see more Cheatham Dam-type projects because of the letter of commendation they received from the Corp of Engineers that testified to their proven success on a major project. Because of these things, Terry and Koski had achieved a greater sense of self-efficacy (*"We can cause good things to happen."*) that came from mastering that massive task.

The Duperon team (Terry and Jim Koski front row, right)

It didn't take long for reality to set in. They were to discover that hunting elephants was much more difficult than hunting squirrels.

Koski got a startling picture of what was to come when he was invited by the Nashville District to give a presentation of the self-cleaning trash rack to engineers representing several southwestern states.

While Koski's presentation went well, it didn't bear any fruit. The major reasons could be attributed to the fact that Hunter Spillum and Traxler had moved on to other projects.

They were still available to help if necessary, but Koski and Terry were left to find other projects with the Corps. They had lost their key sponsors, and Duperon was essentially on its own. This brought Terry and Koski to the stark realization that lacking a champion (like Congressman Traxler) to help them navigate the rough waters from concept to funding to getting a contract to build, future projects would take long periods of time, possibly several years.

Another challenge was the shifting of priorities from storm water to hydropower screening. Storm water comes mainly from ditches — containing leaves, brush, trash, etc. Hydropower comes from rivers — containing large trees, heavy brush, dead animals, etc. Shifting to hydropower would require making more modifications of the trash rack to accommodate sifting out river debris.

Koski went to several hydropower conferences on the east and west coasts and Canada. "We were confident that we could adjust our trash rack to work in the hydropower arena much like we had accomplished with the Cheatham Dam project. However, we were not able to sell this whole new idea. Potential clients were reluctant to take a chance on us."

Duperon did not have the financial reserves to wait for distant payments, so they were surviving on the little cash flow they had to keep the business going and to keep everyone on the payroll.

Perhaps the final straw occurred when Koski scheduled flights to Taipei, Taiwan, and Bagdad, Iraq. There appeared to be strong possibilities in both places. Koski was still in recovery from his cancer surgery but he felt driven to do all that was necessary to secure a contract in either or both of these places.

Koski's first trip would be to Taipei. He and Terry saw this as possibly another Cheatham Dam-type contract. Koski had to fly from Texas to Detroit before he could fly to Taipei. He had just finished presenting to a large contingent of the Corps of Engineers that had scheduled a special sales opportunity for Duperon Corporation based on the success the company had experienced with the Cheatham Dam project. Koski's wife met him at the airport to give him a change of clothing. The next leg of his flight was to

Tokyo, Japan, and it was long and excruciating. As Koski tells it, "There were no business class seats available so I sat with the chickens and ducks." For the remainder of the trip, Koski flew business class. He flew from Tokyo to Okinawa and from Okinawa to Taipei. All of this took place in one day if you account for the twelve-hour time difference between Michigan and Taipei. Upon landing in Taipei, Koski went to the hotel to grab a few hours of badly needed sleep.

According to Koski, "We discovered that the Taiwan Housing and Urban Development people were interested in the trash rack concept we used on the dam. They were extremely nice, hard-working, English-speaking individuals. Surprisingly, they had all adopted American names like Bob, Tom, and Don — probably to spare me the challenge of calling them by their real names and remembering correct pronunciations."

Koski was optimistic early on in their conversations because he could see that there was buy-in. He had visited a stormwater pump station drain. He could see that what they needed was very doable. Finally, Koski got a meeting with the top dog, the head of Federal Housing and Development.

"Oddly, as I stepped off the elevator, there was a big sign of a circle with a slash through it. The sign read 'No Payoffs!' It didn't take long for me to realize that, in fact, payoffs were essential to any contract we would agree to. It was non-negotiable on their side of any agreement. When I computed the deal they were offering, the price jumped from roughly $6 million to $18 million. Terry and I talked and, realizing it was against the law to agree to and pay such bribes to a foreign country, we rejected the deal. Going to jail was not on the radar for either of us. We did offer to sell them our equipment and leave it up to them to charge whatever they wanted internally, but that was the best we had to offer. No deal!"

Terry and Koski faced a very difficult financial future. After working for six years with Terry, and facing the prospect of not getting a paycheck for six months while using his own credit card for travel expenses, Koski decided he had to part ways with the Duperon Corporation. In a negotiation with Terry, they agreed that Koski's departure was probably best for both parties. Terry accepted the responsibility for paying business-related credit card debt that Koski had accrued. In addition, Terry was able to pay one more month of Koski's medical insurance.

Koski and Terry departed as friends. Koski says, "Although things didn't work out entirely as we had hoped, I look at my time working with Terry as a major part of my learning experience in business and I left with absolutely no regrets for the time I spent with Terry and his Duperon Corporation. Given the chance, I would do it all over again. I will never forget that Terry paid me while I was going through my cancer treatments, enabling me to take care of my family."

Terry says, "I loved working with Jim. Of all the cutbacks and reduction in staff I had to make, having Jim decide to leave was the hardest on me. It was emotionally devastating, but it was necessary, and both Jim and I knew it."

18

TEAMWORK MAKES THE DREAM WORK

In 1993, Duperon Corporation appeared to be a sinking ship. Terry was facing severe losses for his business and himself. As Terry says, "I was living my dream — one nightmare at a time."

Tammy, Terry's eldest daughter, was intrigued by the challenge of Terry's business after graduating with her business degree from Saginaw Valley State University. "For years, I listened to my father talk about business and what he was doing. It raised the hairs on the back of my neck. To me it sounded like Russian roulette. I knew that he was behind on billing clients, owed back payroll to employees, and had tax problems. I could feel my anxiety rise and often requested a change of subject."

Tammy began providing consulting services to see if they could find a way forward. She was not paid for her consulting. After a few months, Terry asked Tammy if she would join the company. Tammy accepted, with one caveat.

Tammy says, "When Dad and I agreed to work together, I told him, 'I will join Duperon Corporation, but only as a partner.' I was not going to join a business that I didn't own nor was I willing to do the work of fighting our way out of the dire straits we were in without having ownership."

Soon she joined her father as a partner at Duperon Corporation. Terry was reluctant to do this at first, but realized he was in need of the skills she brought to the business. "I could see from the very beginning that the underpinnings that drive business success were not in place. I began to see that Tammy could bring some management understanding and a strong work ethic at a time when both were desperately needed. It was the next clear thought, so I acted on it."

The early days of working together, using their strengths, and growing in respect for each other.

Tammy continues, "From working with my husband, David, for thirteen years at Bernier Cast Metals, I discovered a love for foundry work and manufacturing. I loved learning about how things work, taking something from an idea and actually making it a physical object that provides value."

According to Terry, "Tammy had always

been an achiever. While at Reese High School, she was class president for all four years, graduated tenth in her class, was homecoming queen, and participated in many extracurricular activities. In high school Tammy clearly showed leadership qualities."

Tammy says, "The thing I loved about working on this with my dad was that we shared values, and loved to imagine futures and invent ways to achieve it. However, it could be difficult, too. Often Dad's ways of operating felt reckless. Having been in the foundry business where cycles were huge, I had learned the benefit of understanding costs, business flows, cash flow, and what made us grow.

"His gifts were in the area of product invention and innovation. My gift is the ability to create business models, structures, and drive outcomes. We had very different ideas about money. I had learned, having been in a highly-cyclical business, to tightly manage cash flow. I was far more frugal. Dad was a creative inventor and a dreamer. I had to learn that this process requires circular paths and time to reiterate and imagine ways around barriers. To Dad, I must have sounded limiting. On the other hand, to me, Dad sounded unreliable and irresponsible.

"The difference between Dad's thinking and mine showed up in the projects Duperon was pursuing and taking, and the poor financial results these projects were producing. I once told him, 'Had I been a part of the Duperon team, I would have strongly advised against the Cheatham Dam project.' He is by far the greater risk taker.

"We began the work of analyzing the business: what made a difference and what did not. Duperon looked to be totally out of control. I started to look at the fundamentals of the business, analyzing projects, and discovering things like warranty issues and uncollected receivables dating as far back as three years. Duperon Corporation was operating in survival mode. Prior to my joining Duperon in 1993, the company had sold the part of the business that provided cash flow."

Tammy shares, "Dad had invented the Duperon Self-Cleaning Trash Rack which seemed to offer hope for profitability. Then, the power industry's mandate to deregulate froze most projects, and we found that the $50 million sales pipeline was actually about $3 million."

Tammy adds, "The fundamental issue was whether or not the company was relevant. Was there a market, [and] with what type of product mix could we cashflow our projects? We needed to reinvent the business. We were out of money, so we needed to quickly figure out if Duperon was capable of surviving."

Duperon's central nervous system challenge was a revenue issue. Terry and Tammy had to determine what type of product(s) they offered and where their market niche was. They needed to gain an in-depth understanding of their products, discover who was going to pay for their products, and how long it would take to collect. All things considered, they were finding out if the business was viable and reliable.

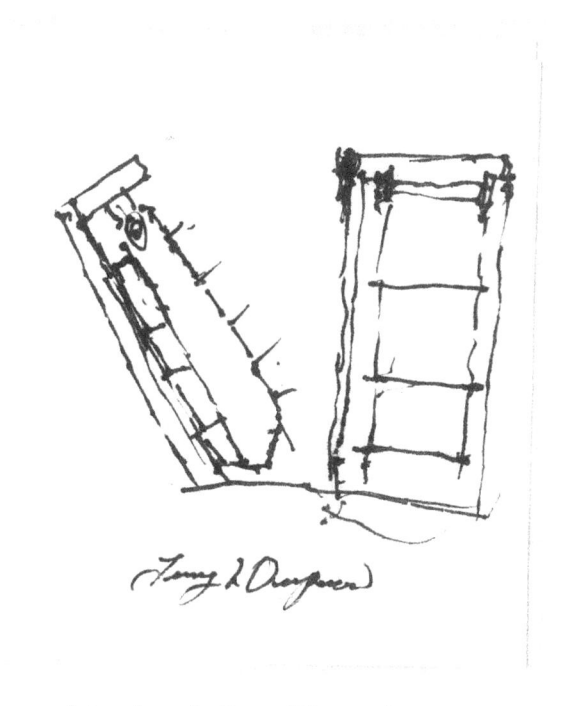

Terry's napkin sketch for a Flex-rake prototype

"Duperon Corporation was under threat to their very existence," Tammy recalls. "The crisis was a clear and present danger. Duperon faced an urgent financial challenge, including the possibility of bankruptcy, the calling in of bank loans, lawsuits, and back pay owed to employees. Dad was rail thin and depressed. We had to find a way."

Terry says, "I was very depressed, but I knew I had to do something besides staying in bed. I went to work on a new product that would have a much lower price point. It was a product that had failed, but I knew how to fix it. I named the new product Flex-rake. It was a completely different product from the self-cleaning trash rack. Because it was less expensive, it could serve a much larger market.

The finished Flex-rake product

"Tammy went to work to assure that Duperon collected any cash owed to it and to get a grip on the amounts of money owed to suppliers and others. In addition, she had to address several open warranty issues."

The fight to save the business was beyond brutal. Tammy shares, "It tested my belief in God, in everything. We were exhausted. It felt like Atlas lifting the earth, and every day provided a new blow to us and the company. Dad was in a very dark place emotionally, facing the imminent possibility of losing all he had worked for. This is where being tough, and having grit, served us well.

"There really was no visible way that the company could be saved — to get out of a million-dollar hole. No clear path. We tried everything. We found we were too poor to go bankrupt (it costs a lot of money!). We tried to sell the company. Finally, we decided to honor the trust given us and do whatever was needed."

Terry was resolutely holding to his conviction that "This company will not die by my hand!" Tammy believed in the adage, "When the need is there, the teacher appears." And for her it came in the form of a book entitled *The E-Myth* by Michael Gerber. "It had amazing lessons like, 'Everyday you are buying or selling your business; make sure it's worth it.'"

The E-Myth was a game-changer for Duperon Corporation. It suggested an exercise that has you think about the end of your life, as you look down from the corner of the room above your coffin, to see what would have made life worth it. Tammy says, "This was an essential question for us as we really had to ask if it was going to be worth trying to save the business — and what could the business be about that would make crawling out of the hole worth it?

"We knew that we needed a goal to shoot for. We wanted to create endless opportunities for our team and to have them fully use their gifts and talents. It was important that we operated with integrity, and that we provided the experience of 'You'll like working with us.' It was important to be a good company — the Tom Bodett of the screening business. Bottom line, though, is we knew that the business, to be worth it, would have to make a difference in the world. Neither of us would count life a success if we didn't."

A powerful team

Tammy continues, "Our agreement was that Dad would design, and I would look at critical issues such as price point and speed of sale. Dad had a product view while I had an operational view. Dad's point of view was, 'We don't have to know all the answers right now.

We just need to start going on a hunt for what to do next.' And I knew that Dad had the ability to do that.

"We made a very powerful team. It took some time to get beyond our differences in how we do business. By allowing each to contribute what we are good at, and intersect at where our abilities and passions were less, we could create a powerful and dynamic catalyst. We have this amazing company that allows people to come in with their gifts and talents and do that again and again. What we know is that, when we work from the best part of ourselves, within our gifts, dreams, and passions, we are unstoppable — a force of nature. It is why we ask people [in job interviews] what their dreams are so that they can see if theirs is located within ours. It is an incredible privilege to be with people who are dedicated to making a difference.

"I think my dream has always been creating what was possible in business. I love making a difference, and figuring out how things work, and how to deliver excellence. In my current role as CEO, when I look at what I can contribute now, I look at such things as:

Can we solve a bigger problem? Can we have a bigger conversation? Can we think of ways to help aspiring entrepreneurs? Can we bring something into the world that doesn't currently exist? Can we create the possibility that we can be unstoppable together?

"My dad created and continues to create a legacy of innovation and invention... but perhaps what he will be most loved for is his ability to see people at their heart, and to hold the space for their dreams."

In the span of three short years, from 1993 through 1996, Duperon Corporation was operating in the black financially. Terry didn't even have a car payment. Terry and Tammy became a productive team that grew Duperon at a rate of about 25 percent per year.

In 2021, Duperon Corporation was awarded the Michigan Manufacturers Innovation Excellence Award by Maner Costerisan. There have been a host of awards over the years (see Appendix). Terry attributes the ability of Duperon Corporation to continually innovate and outclass its competitors to the following: "It comes down to the team and its ability to problem solve."

A proud moment: being named the 2008 Manufacturer of the Year for small businesses.

19

THE "YOU AND ME" CULTURE

Creating a strong culture to drive performance through empowered employees was very important to Terry. He really liked the concept of empowerment — giving people at all levels a voice. Working with Joseph Ofori-Dankwa, a business professor at Saginaw Valley State University, he began to work with a concept called Zero Power Management, which in its purest form takes the authority out of the hands of supervisors, literally doing away with the hierarchy structure of most businesses.

Terry found through experimentation at Duperon that the Zero Power Management approach worked in some cases but in others it failed. Failures in most cases were due to problems encountered when some of the employees used their power for personal gain instead of for the good of the whole. He learned from others who had tried Zero Power Management that they also struggled. Employees looked at their supervisors from the perspective that, while they had removed their guns from their hips, they simply had put the guns in their vests, thereby still retaining the old structure of top-down management.

While Terry retained the belief that employees need to have a voice, some hierarchical structure is still needed to make sure, as Harry Truman once said, "the buck stops here." He meant that supervisors need to retain enough power to ensure accountability in the organization.

At the time that Tammy joined the company, Duperon was down to two full-time people (Terry and Tammy) and a part-time bookkeeper. Zero Power had not worked in some ways, but had provided some great lessons about what is possible when an employee "owned" their position.

Today, on the walls of Duperon Corporation, the poem "Celebrating a Dream" is portrayed in a mural:

> *Each of us has a light,*
> *a gift to be given,*
> *that has been given us.*
> *And, in the eddies*
> *of those vast and inner pools,*
> > *emerges the dream*
> *of the possibility that business*
> *could call forth the best within us.*
> *A dream that celebrates the possi-*
> > *bility of human creativity*
> *and aligned human endeavor.*
> *A dream that, once unleashed*
> *within the minds and hearts of*
> > *people,*
> *becomes a force of nature,*
> *that calls us to good work*
> *with good people (fun to play*
> > *with, too).*
> *Good people*
> *with a heart for service,*
> *who believe in enriching the lives*
> > *of others*

> *and the power of a good deed.*
> *People who grow within*
> > *themselves,*
> *and within others,*
> *the seeds of greatness.*

In Cameron Herold's book *Double Double*, he writes, "When you intersect dreams, passions, talents/skills, and the inherent desire to make a difference, you create a force of nature… a YOU and ME culture."

Tammy reflects, "When people are bringing who they are, what they care about, their dreams, and the desire to make a difference, it *is* a force of nature. It is unstoppable.

"So often in business, we unintentionally create power structures, and other types of dynamics that become an ecosystem of survival. It creates destructive behaviors and is grounded in a win/lose proposition. Positioning for power, trying to be seen as the one getting credit, making others look bad, hiding, and information-withholding are some of the characteristics of this environment. There is 'only so much' and you have to compete to get 'it.'

"Duperon's 'You and Me' culture is an environment where people can authentically be themselves. This dissipates much of the friction so common to many business cultures. Our intention at Duperon is to each share our gifts so that people know who we are, what we value, how it shows up in the world, and the impact it makes." The walls of Duperon are filled with quotes and inspiration that reflect this goal:

> *You will like working with us.*
> *Team Duperon daring to make a difference. For people. For Water. For the Planet.*
> *We love to WOW our customers.*
> *Imagine if...*
> *Celebrating the Dream*

The Test of Culture

A real test of a powerful culture is how well it navigates through the hard times brought on by external challenges that can easily uproot a company's success and profitability. One such challenge was the economic recession that lasted from December 2007 through June 2009. A second challenge was the coronavirus pandemic of 2020.

Both of these external challenges impacted international corporations, Fortune 500 companies, and small entrepreneurial businesses. All of these companies faced big decisions that would determine their demise and death or the brightness of their future. Decisions had to be made and they had to be made fast.

The Recession

The recession led to the demise of many businesses. Duperon Corporation survived and advanced through it. To gain an understanding of how Duperon Corporation managed to survive and advance, it is important to refer to a blog article on the *Mlive.com* news website by Terry Duperon (May 7, 2009), "In These Hard Economic Times." What Terry had to say is very provocative:

In these hard economic times, I'm starting to see three basic approaches.

The Fixer looks at his situation in a very realistic way. "If it's broken, fix it." If there is less money, cut back and tighten our belts until the economy gets better.

The Wisher looks at his situation and says, "We must think positive. Don't let negative thoughts creep in!" If there is a recession, we don't have to join it. Something will come along and make it all better.

But the Innovator looks at his situation and asks, "What's the dream?" In other words, what is the idea that you have faith in but don't know how to accomplish? The Innovator knows that innovation lives under the umbrella of the dream, and if he pursues the dream, the "how-to" always shows itself.

The Innovator is also a Wisher and a Fixer, but with these differences: The Wisher and the Fixer look outside themselves for things to get better; the Innovator does not. The Innovator turns his wish into a dream, which he champions, and is thus able to cause it to happen. He fixes only the things that he needs to — to cause the dream to happen.

There once was a wagon train. It was moving along nicely until one day it hit a rock and broke the spokes out of a wheel. The Fixer said, "We have methods, processes, and systems to fix the wheel!"

The Wisher said, "Something will come along and we will be just fine."

The Innovator asked, "What's the dream? Where are we going?"

The dream is to get to California. We are at the foothills of the mountain. We need to go up. We don't need a wheel. We don't need a wagon. We need a rope.

When Terry was asked about Duperon's approach to successfully dealing with the recession, he had this to say: "We kept the mindset that we were not going to join the recession and we were going to continue to grow this business in spite of the current downfall of the economy. This mindset caused us to see opportunities for innovation and growth. The opposite were business leaders who operated out of fear, and began to see opportunities for staff reductions, cutting travel, and other things that aligned with their mindset.

"We had good leaders. Our culture was great. The employees believed in our leadership, and this reduced or eliminated the anxiety and stress that accompany the fear-based approach."

The Duperon Corporation team in 2014

Tammy's insight on how the Duperon Corporation made it through the recession is,

"In our line of business, we are funded for a project two to three years before the project starts, so we had ongoing projects in the pipeline. This meant that we would be impacted later and we needed to see the opportunities now. Our great team and culture was another contributing factor because the ability to trust one another and move with confidence and caring makes the difference. Had we agreed to be a part of the recession, we would have been accepting that as the absolute truth, and that would have limited what we could see and felt was possible."

In 2016, it was time for another change. After a significant year of personal challenge and the death of Mike Pruitt, a good friend and Duperon's marketing director, a significant opportunity emerged. Tammy remembers, "It was completely unexpected and, for me, another one of those 'God things.'" A colleague who was being groomed to succeed as CEO in a competitive firm was making a change. Tammy and Mark Turpin had both been in Water and Wastewater Equipment Manufacturers Association (WWEMA), a national trade organization, where Tammy was the current chair and he was the chair-elect.

"I had known Mark Turpin for years and had always been impressed by, not only how smart he was, but also the integrity with which he always operated," Tammy shared. "When Mark became available, I indicated immediately that we would be interested in speaking with him. Mark is extraordinary and while our culture was very different from the more corporate experiences he had, the values alignment was right on."

The rest is history: Terry remained chairman of the board with Tammy as CEO, and Mark Turpin became the president and accountable for the operations of the organization. Tammy says, "Mark is outstanding and we are grateful for the opportunity we have been given to create something together. He adapted quickly to the culture. The team grew. He is the perfect leader for this time in our company. He is systematic and helps drive incremental growth within the team, products, and innovation. He is consistent and is a vital leader and member of the team." Both

Terry and Tammy are grateful on so many levels for Mark's contribution.

COVID-19 Pandemic

On February 25, 2020, the Center for Disease Control announced that COVID-19 was heading toward a pandemic. President Donald Trump declared the novel coronavirus a national emergency on March 13, 2020. (Ironically, superstition says that Friday the 13th is known as an unlucky day.)

When COVID-19 first reared its head, Terry says, "I thought it was like any other flu. I didn't believe it would turn into a pandemic. When the pandemic became apparent, there were many decisions that had to be made.

"By this time, Mark was entrenched as president of Duperon Corporation. Tammy and Mark began meeting one or two times per week to strategize how Duperon Corporation would deal with what was happening." Tammy adds, "Mark also did not make any decisions that were not needed and might preclude another decision from being made when more information was available. He and

I wrestled with the scenarios in the background so as to not cause confusion or more uncertainty for those who had to act with confidence. 'What would happen if we could not work at all? Would we have to furlough everyone? What kind of reserves did we have? What if our customers and/or suppliers could not work?' These were all unanswered for all businesses, but the company's values and culture made certain things absolutely clear, and thankfully we were all aligned. We would try to get as many of our teams and stakeholders to the other side as we could, as safe as possible. We felt that if the worst happened, we would attempt to maintain insurance for as long as we could to make sure our team was not financially exposed during a time when their families could be most vulnerable.

"We wrestled with being conservative with resources so that we could do the best we could for everyone. We assured our employees that workers who had to quarantine due to exposure or travel would not bear those costs. We also started looking at our suppliers and our independent reps to see if they would experience specific cashflow or material challenges. We followed the mandates and requirements of the state, not because we agreed with everything (we, like everyone, had opinions!), but that, as a company with a core value of integrity, we would follow the rules. And even beyond them, and often before those mandates, we would make decisions that would best support our team and all the people depending on us.

"Our culture drives our success. For example, our IT team had been advocating for the Microsoft Teams platform for months. They were certain that this capability would help the company perform. Mark and I were less certain. Our IT team had a voice and thank goodness they did. IT went from a pilot [program] with a few users to having delivered the program to the entire company within forty-eight hours. It was incredible watching our IT team pull this off.

"Also, our culture of caring for one another provided an atmosphere wherein people worked together in search of ways to successfully grapple with both their home and work situations. Being committed to serving each other and being grateful made a difference for everyone. We even had our independent sales partners state that Duperon was one of the best, if not *the* best, in working together through this time of uncertainty and in taking care of customers."

There is a moment during this pandemic that Tammy says she will never forget. "Larry, our operations manager, posted a picture of the first loaded truck after the pandemic shutdown, with a copy of the letter from the customer declaring us 'essential' workers, and that if they had not received this equipment in May, they would not be able to meet their community's infrastructure demands for wastewater management. I felt like it was our version of 'hoisting the flag on Iwo Jima.' To be able to serve, to matter, to make a difference, and to have managed each and every thing needed to do so… it doesn't get better than that."

This is where culture pays off. Tammy says, "When you know who you are, you know what to do. By having a team with shared values for making a difference, work becomes a place where we get to be the way we always dreamed of being. We will look back at this pandemic and marvel about what we learned and who we are now, because of this challenge."

The "You and Me" culture at Duperon Corporation has survived and advanced through many challenges that would have destroyed businesses with a lesser culture. Each subsequent challenge appears to add to their cultural success bank.

20

THE CLASS

Terry's current passion is helping others achieve their dreams. To do this, he has created what he calls *The CLASS*. Terry gave this a very simple name because, as he has learned, his creativity does not extend to product names. He tends to be very literal. For example, Terry's marketing director said that if Terry had invented sushi, he would have called it "cold dead fish."

The CLASS is an outgrowth of an unlikely experience: Terry was asked to speak to a senior engineering class at Saginaw Valley State University. Terry says, "Professor Tom Caldron invited me to teach a class about entrepreneurship. We were both serving on the Michigan Manufacturers Association Board at that time. He must have assumed that I was an engineer. I am sure he had no idea that I didn't know how to read or write beyond about the third-grade level or that I had no college education. As a matter of fact, I had never even visited a college campus before.

"They should have done their homework and realized they were asking a high school dropout to teach college engineering students. Fortunately, they did know that I was an entrepreneur.

"I was hesitant at first, but I decided to try teaching the class because I had made a promise that I would never be the one to limit myself. When I walked into the classroom that first day, I thought, 'What am I doing here? I have no idea how to be a professor,' but because of the promise I had made to myself, I knew I had to try."

Terry decided to arrive an hour early to give himself time to grow accustomed to being there. He knew how difficult it would be for himself. The school environment was always a place of trauma for him, and his body showed the signs of it — even the smell of chalk made him feel ill.

"When I taught my first class, I put the entire group in a coma. I tried to act like a professor and quickly realized I had no idea of how to do that. Fortunately, after that first class I got some coaching from a teacher friend of mine. She said, 'The most important thing is to know your audience and simply tell your story of what got you to where you are today.' It became clear to me that the only thing that separated me from the students in my class was the way I think. I hoped that if I could share my way of thinking with the senior engineering students, I would inspire them to dream big dreams and trust that the 'how' to achieve their dream would show itself. This would shift the students into living in a mood of inquiry." The seed was planted for the seminar Terry now calls *The CLASS*.

The CLASS is a curriculum that has been developed and refined over many years to encompass basic entrepreneurial skill sets that anyone can use: the ability to see and hear opportunity, take productive action, and create something new. The course grew from Terry

Duperon's experiences with invention and innovation within Duperon Corporation. It helps participants identify their personal dreams and make them happen.

In *The CLASS*, Terry shares his life's story, and credits his transformation from being a misfit in school to becoming a wealthy entrepreneur and business owner to what might be called the inventor's mindset: the thought process of an entrepreneur, which is the never-ending quest to bring something into this world that does not exist now.

This inventor's mindset is at the core of Terry's way of being and has resulted in his achieving multiple patents. Through *The CLASS*, Terry draws from his own experiences at bringing new things into this world through stories and anecdotes that open up whole new worlds of possibility for his seminar participants.

"The message at the core of *The CLASS* is, 'Pursue your passion, the dream that feeds you.' Your dream can be a very vague notion of something that brings out the best in the person God made you to be."

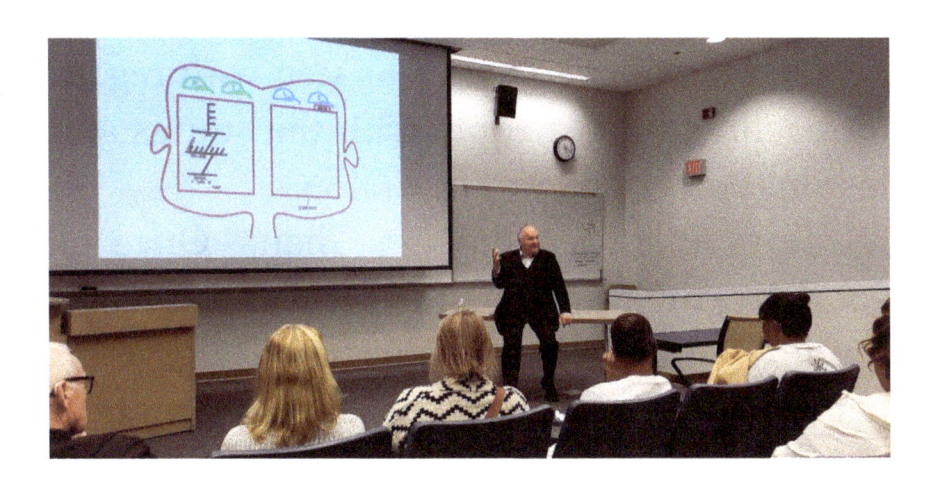

Once Terry saw the positive effects *The CLASS* had on his senior engineering students, he decided to offer it to friends and family. For the past eighteen years, he has presented *The CLASS* to hundreds of participants, ranging across the spectrum of ages, socio-economic positions in life, and widely-differing aspirations. For many, *The CLASS* has been a life-changing experience.

Terry took *The CLASS* international after he was approached by SVSU professor Joseph Ofori-Dankwa. Ofori-Dankwa asked if Terry would be willing to go to Ghana, Africa, and teach *The CLASS* at a university, offer *The CLASS* to a group of aspiring young wannabe-entrepreneurs, and speak to his church congregation. It took Terry two years to decide if a trip to Africa made sense. It was then that he decided it was the next clear step with regard to reaching more people with the stories and lessons embedded in *The CLASS*.

Terry spent ten days in Ghana. Once he got there, the purpose of his trip expanded to training others to teach his class. He gave his participant manual to those who are now trained to offer *The CLASS* to others.

While in Ghana, he met King Osagyefuo Amoatia Ofori Panin Okyenhene and other high-ranking officials. He also met a woman named Priscilla, who is a teacher of autistic children. She loved *The CLASS* and indicated a strong interest in knowing more about dyslexia. Terry paid for Priscilla to come to Saginaw and SVSU arranged the trip so she could get training on dyslexia. Priscilla is now taking her newly-acquired dyslexia knowledge across the country of Ghana.

The participants of *The CLASS* in Ghana (Priscilla is front row, right.)

Terry's trip to Ghana was Ofori-Dankwa's dream, not Terry's. Terry's new passion is helping others like Priscilla and Ofori-Dankwa realize the true potential of having a dream and following it by taking one clear step at a time. More trips to Ghana are being planned.

Recently, Terry had *The CLASS* recorded so that it can be offered to a much broader audience. Using up-to-date technology, participants are able to access all the units and review them over and over again. There are self-check assessments and exercises that support the learning process.

Terry's reach in Saginaw and beyond continues to expand. In Saginaw, Terry serves on the board of the Dyslexic Foundation and is a member of the Blue Angels Investor Group in Bay City, Michigan. He teaches and coaches aspiring entrepreneurs and enlists business personnel to invest in the dreams of aspiring entrepreneurs.

21

THE PURSUIT OF HAPPINESS

The bird a nest, the spider a web, man friendship.

— William Blake

The ancient Greeks defined four levels of happiness:

1. Instant gratification: This first level of happiness comes with intense feeling and is always temporary, i.e., see the ice cream — eat the ice

cream. If we rely on instant gratification, we will always feel unfulfilled and never satisfied.
2. Competition: This level of happiness requires us to see ourselves as having to be bigger than, better than, or more than anyone else. In every encounter, we are measuring ourselves against the other person or group. When we feel "better than," we feel superior or have contempt toward the other person or group. The problem with this level of happiness is that we will always find someone or some group better than us. If we derive our happiness from competition, we walk around only looking for people we see ourselves as "better than."
3. Contribution: In finding happiness through contribution, we are looking for ways to use our time and talents to help and support others. We derive joy from improving the human condition —

giving a boost to someone else's dream or repairing the damage done by neglect, injury, or handicap. We don't need attention or recognition. The very act of giving of ourselves by creatively coming up with solutions brings a level of satisfaction and happiness that carries no expectation of personal reward or recognition.

4. The seeking of ultimate perfection: In finding happiness at this level, we are seeking ultimate perfection, perfect love, perfect beauty, ultimate knowledge. This level is the most difficult to reach because perfection is fleeting — if possible at all. We may only experience moments, but we humans are dreamers, goal-seekers; we strive to get as close to perfection as we can.

Terry Duperon, like many of us, achieved some degree of happiness in a combination of all of these levels. In my work as a psychologist, I've found that, at a very basic level, *hap-*

piness is simply a feeling which we can get by either giving or getting: we want the new baby, the new car, the new house because of the feeling of happiness they give us. We like to receive presents and awards. The problem is, we can't control how much we get in life. On the other hand, happiness can be achieved by giving. The happiness benefit of giving is best because we can control how much we give, whether it's simply a smile to someone who is lonely or a start-up loan to chase one's dream. The feeling of happiness in both cases is the same. In the end, the only thing we keep forever is what we give away.

Terry is a dream weaver for others, and through his entrepreneurship, he is in control of his giving, and therefore his happiness. He is sharing his dream through *The CLASS* and then sharing the thought processes that propelled him to success and happiness.

Terry has turned the reins of running the Duperon Corporation over to Mark Turpin. While he still serves as chairman of the board for Duperon Corporation, this dreamer is now dedicated to helping others achieve their dreams by teaching *The CLASS,* providing start-up funding, and mentoring aspiring entrepreneurs.

Reflecting on his career, Terry says "I haven't worked in forty-three years! I love my life, I love my wife. What else could I possibly ask for?" Terry's expression of loving the life he is living is expressed beautifully in Alan Jackson's song, "The Older I Get":

> *The older I get*
> *The more I think*
> *You only get a minute, better live while you're in it*
> *'Cause it's gone in a blink*
> *And the older I get*
> *The truer it is*
> *It's the people you love, not the money and stuff*
> *That makes you rich*
>
> *And if they found a fountain of youth*
> *I wouldn't drink a drop and that's the truth*
> *Funny how it feels I'm just getting to my best years yet*

The older I get
The fewer friends I have
But you don't need a lot when the
    ones you got
Have always got your back
And the older I get
The better I am
At knowing when to give
And when to just not give a damn

And I don't mind all the lines
From all the times I've laughed
    and cried
Souvenirs and little signs of the
    life I've lived

And the older I get
The more I pray
I don't know why, I guess that I've
Got more to say
And the older I get
The more thankful I feel
For the life I've lived and the life
    I'm living still

APPENDIX

Terry Duperon is chairman of the board of Duperon Corporation, an international company that designs, develops, and manufactures preliminary liquids/solids separation technologies for dams, pump stations, wastewater, and industrial applications.

Duperon Corporation has been recognized with Saginaw Future's Economic Excellence Award (2005, 2006, 2007, 2012, 2013); Michigan's 50 Companies to Watch (2006); Michigan Export Achievement Award (2007); Corp! Magazine Michigan Economic Bright Spot Award (2008); Michigan Manufacturer of the Year (2008); Corp! Magazine Best of Michigan Business (2011); Saginaw Future's Outstanding Investment in Saginaw County (2014); and by the Mid-Michigan Innovation Center for Innovation and Leadership to Enhance the Michigan Entrepreneurial Environment (2014); Succession Success Award—Best of MichBusiness Awards and Gala (2017).

In 2009, Terry Duperon was inducted into the Junior Achievement Business Hall of Fame for his role in mentoring and inspiring community youth. In 2010, Terry Duperon was recognized with the Dr. Samuel H. Shaheen Vision of Free Enterprise Award, as well as the Corp! Magazine Entrepreneur of Distinction Award. In 2011, Terry Duperon was honored as a semi-finalist in the Ernst & Young Entrepreneur of the Year Awards. In 2016, Terry Duperon was selected as the recipient of the Achievement Award by Women of Colors in recognition of demonstrated excellence in business leadership and his ability to mentor and inspire local youth and entrepreneurs. In 2017, he was recognized by the Saginaw Valley State University College of Business and Management with their Outstanding Entrepreneur Award.

Terry Duperon's four decades in business have led to a non-traditional approach to viewing opportunity and the development of Duperon Education, a curriculum born of his experiences with invention and innovation at Duperon Corporation. The curriculum encompasses basic entrepreneurial skills that anyone is able to access and use. In 2018 this was proven true, as Terry was invited to bring Duperon Education to the PALI New Year Entrepreneurship school in Ghana, Africa, where he taught young entrepreneurs strategies for creative thinking and innovation. Employees of Duperon Corporation are encouraged to participate in the class and use entrepreneurial innovation in their jobs.

The holder of five patents, Mr. Duperon utilizes the skills of entrepreneurship and innovation daily. He has taught entrepreneurial skills to senior engineers at Saginaw Valley State University and is the author of *A Different Ability* and *Dare to Be Different.*

He is a member of the Michigan Manufacturer's Association as well as the Saginaw Valley Manufacturer's Association, where he served as a board member and also as president. He is also involved with the NFIB, the Saginaw Chamber of Commerce, and the SERA Club. He is a member of the Saginaw Club Board of Directors, a board member of Junior Achievement, and sits on the board of governors of The Children's Dyslexia Centers, Inc. Mr. Duperon also participates in the Cardinal Formula Racing (CFR) Advisory Committee.

Terry Duperon has written a recurring blog column for MLive Business, and has presented to distinguished local groups such as the Saginaw County Teachers Association, SVSU Family Business Program, Delta College Entrepreneurship Program, and the Bay City Chamber of Commerce. In 2015, he presented the annual Toast to the Office of the President at the Saginaw Club.

ABOUT THE AUTHOR

Donald J. Steele, Jr., PhD, is a man of many talents and passions. He earned his PhD from The Ohio State University and his multifaceted career started first in the field of education where he served as Superintendent of Schools in three urban school districts: Saginaw, Michigan; Toledo, Ohio; and Seattle, Washington. Don then put his PhD in psychology to work as an optimal performance coach working with organizations as diverse as the NFL, Microsoft, NASCAR, and Ford Motor Company. All along, Don made time to pursue his passion for song writing, performing, and recording music. He recorded duet albums with Tammy Wynette and Willie Nelson among other musical accomplishments. Most recently, Don serves as an adjunct professor at Saginaw Valley State University and is authoring legacy books about family-owned and operated businesses and entrepreneurial endeavors. For inquiries about capturing your life story in a legacy book, please check out *performance-learninginc.com*.

ACKNOWLEDGMENTS

A very special thanks goes out to Julie Mall, whose expertise in editing extended far beyond dotting i's and crossing t's. She freely contributed her thoughts as she reviewed both content and style. She is acutely aware of how important the flow of information is to make it easy for the reader to follow and look forward to what's to come. I have already engaged her services in the books I'm currently writing.

Terry Duperon and Tammy Bernier, his daughter and long-time business partner, gave freely of their time and talents to ensure that I got the information I needed when I needed it. The entire Duperon family, starting with Leslie and all of their children, were also very helpful in the process of contributing information that added to this body of work.

Jim Koski, formerly Terry's business partner, played an important role in the development of Terry's business early on. The acuity of his memories, accompanied with pictures that captured historical events, were very important to this book.

John Murray, the brother of Jackie Duperon, Terry's first wife, was very forthright in his insights of their upbringing and gave us access to information not available anywhere else.

I also want to thank those people who were willing to be interviewed, sharing their thoughts about their interactions in Terry Duperon's personal and business life.

With Special Assistance

Mackenzie Morris, a recent Summa Cum Laude (4.0 grade-point average) graduate of the Carmona College of Business at Saginaw Valley State University, contributed valuable time to reviewing content and suggesting improvements. It has been a pleasure to work with Saginaw Valley State University students like Mackenzie because they bring new perspectives to almost any circumstance.

Printed in the USA
CPSIA information can be obtained
at www.ICGtesting.com
JSHW010055040823
45790JS00004B/12/J